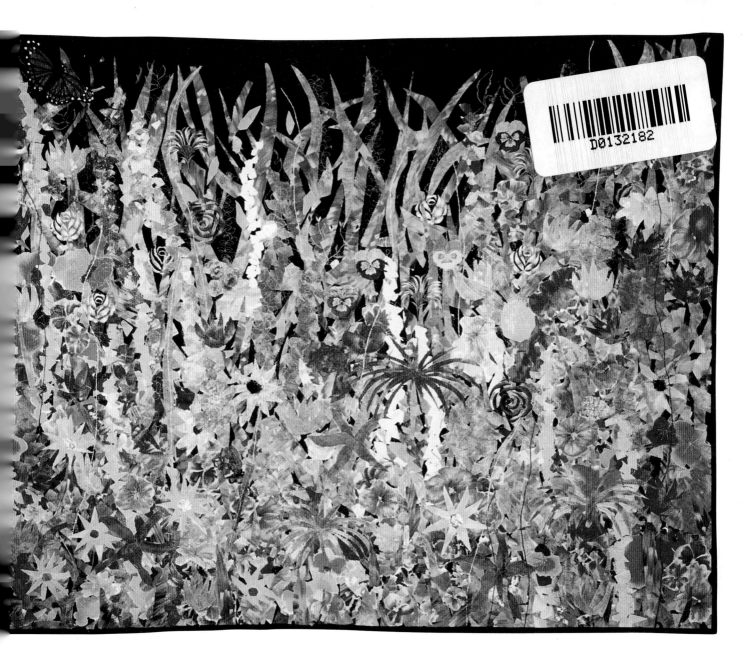

Contemporary
Quilting

Exciting Techniques and Quilts from Award-Winning Quilters

By Cindy Walter and Stevii Graves

©2005 Cindy Walter and Stevii Graves
Published by

kp books
An Imprint of F+W Publications

700 East State Street • Iola, WI 54990-0001
715-445-2214 • 888-457-2873

Our toll-free number to place an order or obtain
a free catalog is (800) 258-0929.

Library of Congress Catalog Number: 2004113668

ISBN: 0-87349-749-X

Edited by Susan Sliwicki and Nicole Gould
Designed by Elizabeth Krogwold

Printed in China

Table of Contents

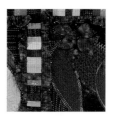

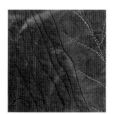
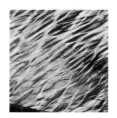

Introduction

"Contemporary Quilting" co-authors (from left) Stevii Graves and Cindy Walter.

The two of us have witnessed a remarkable evolution in quilting over the past 20 years. Everything has changed. Take rotary equipment as one example. The realization that there is a whole new generation of quilters who never had to cut out a quilt top with scissors was inspiration enough for us to write this book.

We interviewed many of the most influential people in the quilting industry to give you their observations and to document the evolution of contemporary quilting. We're sure you'll find this first section of the book exciting and informative. We've also included 12 step-by-step projects so you can try your hand at some newer techniques. The book closes with a glorious gallery of stunning quilts made by some of the most talented quilt makers in the world. Many of the designers whose quilts are featured in the gallery are available to teach their art, so we've listed their contact information in a source list for your convenience.

We'd like to thank our families and friends for their constant support over the past two years, especially Michael A. Lilly and Randy Graves. We'd also like to thank the hundreds of people we interviewed, all of whom were so generous with their time and information. We especially give a huge thank-you to Karey Bresenhan and Donna Wilder, who were extremely generous with their precious time and knowledge. And because there were so many people involved in quilting over the past decades, we'd like to acknowledge that this is just a sampling of the companies and talented artists who have made contributions to the quilt world.

We hope you enjoy this peek into the world of contemporary quilting.

Cindy Walter
Stevii Graves

The Evolution of Contemporary Quilting

Part 1

When we began the research for this book, we knew there were several explanations for the evolution of contemporary quilting; we just didn't realize there were so many factors tessellating together to create the big picture. Every aspect of quilting has played a role: new notions, innovative tools, exciting fabric designs and modern technology ranging from computerized sewing machines to the Internet. Most importantly, the average quilter no longer was afraid to think outside the box.

Stevii Graves recalls how her heart sang when she first saw the show catalog in 1990 for the Visions exhibition in San Diego. She thought about how bed quilts warm the body, but these contemporary wall quilts warm the spirit. She was so enthralled with the Vision quilts that contemporary quilts and techniques soon became her passion. In 1992, she became the president of Quilt Visions and edited two of their exhibition catalogs.

Cindy Walter recalled wanting to paint on her quilts in the early 1990s. At the time, she was teaching only traditional quilting techniques, and her friends thought painting on a quilt was an awful idea. When she invented the Snippet Sensations® fusible art technique, she had to force some of her friends to make snippet projects for her first book. Since there were no books written at the time on fusible web art quilts, some of them thought these projects were not really quilts but rather some form of pop art. Little did they realize that the world was primed for this new contemporary technique. The first print run of "Snippet Sensations" sold out in about a month, and the book continues to sell in dozens of countries. The world certainly views the art of quilting differently now than it did just a decade ago.

It would be impossible to list every quilter who played a role in the changes we've witnessed. It seems that quilters in every corner of the United States and the world broke out of the traditional mold at about the same time. For your inspiration, several of these creative quilters have lent us quilts for the gallery section of this book.

The companies in our industry were a major encouragement to these quilters. We were able to interview representatives of several companies and reflect in this section their observations of the improvements their companies have made to keep up with the ever-changing quilting world. Most of the companies have interesting Web sites, which are listed in the Resources section, that contain a veritable flood of information and even free patterns.

After Karey Bresenhan founded the first wholesale quilt market 30 years ago, the event became a major factor in the evolution of quilting. Because of this convention, shop owners from around the United States and eventually the world were able to purchase new and exciting products and fabrics, which in turn inspired many quilters to reach new levels. The market also allowed quilters to have direct contact with manufacturers, which in turn encouraged companies to make better products.

Stevii Graves, "Journal Quilt," 8 ½" x 11". In 2002, Karey Bresenhan invited members of the online group Quiltart to make monthly journal quilts as part of a special exhibit for the International Quilt Association in Houston. This is one of several panels Graves made for her quilt about her fight against cancer.

Bresenhan also founded the huge International Quilt Festival, held annually in both Houston and Chicago, and the Patchwork and Quilt Expo, held every two years in Europe. These large consumer shows bring people together from all over the world to see the Festival quilt exhibits.

These annual quilt shows are truly trendsetters and are ones you won't want to miss. Some of the current trends in quilt making, like journal quilts, began with special exhibits at the International

"The International Quilt Market is the world's only trade show specifically serving the quilting industry. It keeps up with changes so that the quilters can find the supplies and inspiration they need when they visit their local quilt stores. At our shows, we showcase special exhibits featuring the best of contemporary quilt making, because these exhibits give manufacturers a chance to see how their products are used and provide opportunities for developing new products to help quilters produce their masterpieces. Also, these exhibits expose quilting retailers and teachers to new trends to share with the quilters from their areas, and seeing these exhibits helps them to recognize quality and artistry in quilts that break with tradition, such as fused quilts, painted quilts and quilts that depend more on surface embellishment than they do on piecing or appliqué. Many of today's quilts are a far cry from our grandmothers' wonderful old scrap quilts. I sometimes wonder if our quilting ancestors came back to Earth for a day whether they would even recognize some of the quilts as quilts, because that's how much quilting has advanced since the last quarter of the 20th century. Quilts provide a tangible link to the past, to generations of women and men who used their needle, thread and fabrics to create comfort for their families and beauty for the beholder. But the quilts also provide a bridge to the future, when residents of tomorrow's technological world will need the simple joy of touching something real rather than virtual, the challenge of the enormous range of nature's colors rather than the computer's limited range, and the comfort of the tactile qualities of quilts."

— *Karey Bresenhan, president of Quilts Inc., director of the wholesale International Quilt Market and director of the consumer International Quilt Festival and Patchwork and Quilt Expo in Europe*

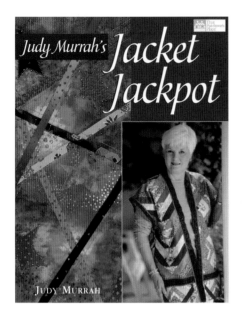

In the early 1990s, contemporary quilting techniques began to appear in wearables, such as vests and jackets. "Jacket Jazz" and "Jacket Jackpot" author Judy Murrah made the trend hot when she combined a variety of quilting techniques on one jacket. She has made wearables for more than 12 years.

Quilt Festival and the Patchwork and Quilt Expo. The shows' exhibits also have commemorated historic and sad events and showed the ways that quilters express their happiness, sorrow or anger through their quilts.

Donna Wilder served as coordinator for the famous Fairfield Fashion Show when she worked for Fairfield Processing Corp. The event, now known as the Bernina Fashion Show, is held annually at the International Quilt Market and Festival.

"Jan Myer Newbury and Nancy Crow are some of the names that come to mind when I think of the original fashion designers," Wilder said. "In the beginning we had to hunt for garments. It wasn't long before wearable art took off, and we had to jury the entries."

Contemporary quilting has taken the art form in new directions, according to Judy Murrah, the director of education for the International Quilt Market and Festival.

"The first show started with only 12 classes and mainly offered hand-working classes, such as hand piecing or quilting. As the wholesale market grew and new products were invented, such as rotary cutters and rulers, quilting went into a new direction," Murrah said. "Now, even computers are used to design quilts. The majority of classes offered at Market and Festival are of contemporary techniques, but traditional classes are always offered and popular."

Although we feel that the International Quilt Market was a major factor in introducing quilters to new products, we also have to give credit to the distribution companies in the field. Their representatives ensured that shop owners who couldn't attend market still were exposed to the array of new products.

Today's quilters demand quality tools to accomplish their goals, said Rob Krieger, president of Checker Distributors. The wholesale company,

Diana Leone, "Returning to my Village," 63" x 48", 1998. This quilt is a tribute to the people of Vietnam. Rob Krieger, president of Checker Distributors, visited this village to mark the 20th anniversary of when he initially returned to the United States from Vietnam. He loved the people and the land, and he expressed his feelings about Vietnam to quilt maker Diana Leone so she could capture the image and give it back to him to enjoy daily. This quilt used a sliced version of her "Crazy with Cotton" technique. Leone has a degree in art and education from San Jose State University. Her training and artistic talent are reflected in her stunning quilts. In the private collection of Rob Krieger, president, Checker Distributors.

which began in 1948, stocks more than 80,000 items to provide one-stop shopping for independent retailers.

"We search the world looking for new products to assist today's quilter," he said. "We've seen lots of improvement of old products and a spirit of entrepreneurship in this exciting business of creating new products."

Quilters have left their mark on the industry, too. "Because quilters are the most creative people in the world, the face of quilting has changed the look of home decor and ready-to-wear," said Jennie Brockman, Checker's book and gift buyer.

Tools and Notions

Many tools and notions played vital roles in the evolution of contemporary techniques. Take rotary equipment, for example. The first rotary cutter was an Olfa product for cutting paper. The blade had a series of numbers near the edge. When one area became dull, you simply moved the blade to the next number. It was not meant to rotate while you cut.

Once the rotating-blade cutter was created, quilters quickly started using it, which, in turn, created the demand for rulers and cutting mats.

In 1985, Peggy Schafer's husband created an acrylic ruler in his workshop, which she took to her quilting bee. Her quilting friends immediately deluged her husband with requests for the new tool, and the Omnigrid ruler was born.

Omnigrid ruler founder Peggy Schafer showcases her rulers at the 2004 International Spring Quilt Market.

People in different parts of the United States began designing their own varying styles of rulers. Marilyn Doheny created a 9-degree circle wedge ruler to cut pieces for beautiful fan quilts. Marti Michell, Kaye Wood and Donna Poster also designed rulers.

"My husband, Arn, began developing and producing a wholesale line of rulers in the '80s," Donna Poster recalled. "At trade shows, one group of ladies routinely scolded him for encouraging the use of this dreadful tool! When the rotary cutter became popular, many long-time quilters were incensed. Their quilts had taken many months to complete, and they insisted that any quilt made in just weeks or days was not a real quilt! It took a number of years, but, as we all know, the rotary cutter is now one of our favorite pieces of equipment!"

Marti Michell of Michell Marketing demonstrates her popular templates at the International Spring Quilt Market 2004, accompanied by her husband, Dick Michell. She has sold more than 1 million books and 1 million patterns.

Marti Michell, founder of Michell Marketing, was an early template designer. She received the 2004 Silver Star Award, which is presented annually to a living person whose body of work has positively influenced, promoted and developed the art of quilting.

"Is it that the quilting community asks and the business community supplies, or vice versa?" Michell asked. "Either way, the current endless variety of quilting styles, methods and fabrics was unimaginable 30 years ago."

Kaye Wood, host of the TV program "Kaye's Quilting Friends," primarily makes traditional quilts, but she uses a very contemporary fashion of speed cutting the pieces with her special rulers. If you've ever seen her cut out a pattern on her show, you'll know what we are talking about. Wood's first template inventions in 1982 were designed as guides for tracing with a pencil. She later redesigned them for use with rotary cutters.

"I think of myself as a 'quilt engineer.' I set out to solve the problems that quilters complain about, whether it is a technique or a project. I designed the Starmaker® rulers after realizing that the same angles were used over and over again in quilt making. Only the size of the piece changes, so a master template can cut any size piece," Wood said.

Products from other countries also have played a role in contemporary quilting. Many quilters first think of Clover Needlecraft Inc., whose parent company is based in Japan, as one such international contributor.

"Quilting today, although continuing to be traditional in nature, has evolved into works of art as well as heirloom projects that will be passed on to relatives for keepsakes. At Clover, our task is to continue bringing new, unique and different products that make a project easier to put together. We all have less time to devote to our hobbies and must make every second count," said Louis Carson, Clover's national account manager.

The Colonial Needle Company imports its high-quality needles from England. American importers Jim Collingham and Terry Collingham developed a chart so quilters can identify the correct hand sewing needles for their tasks.

"Needles have evolved to fit the demands, including large-eyed hand quilting needles and ballpoint embroidery needles to add beads to quilts," they said.

The Bohin Needle Factory was established in 1869 in Normandy, France.

The Bohin Company, which built its needle factory in 1869 in Normandy, France, makes many products in addition to needles. Surprisingly, the company still uses some of the factory's original machines. But it also has worked to keep pace with industry needs.

"In the past few years, as we have been seeing more art quilts, we have developed new products to meet the quilters' demands. Quilters wanted a longer, thinner pin, and, of course, a thinner needle with a large eye. We also created a chalk marker with a lot of different colors of chalk to show up on all types of fabrics for the contemporary quilter," said Didier Vrac, Bohin president, and Jerome Doussard, marketing director.

When fusible web came onto the market about 20

Fusible web has helped to expand quilters' creative options.

years ago, it opened new possibilities to quilters. Many of us feel that this was an important revelation.

In the mid-1990s, "Contemporary Quilting" co-author Cindy Walter was resting in bed, dreaming about painting on her quilts. The idea came to her in the wee hours: put fusible web on the back of the "palette" fabric and simply cut pieces for a pictorial project. Snippet Sensations was born.

The invention of Steam-A-Seam2 fusible web in 1995 enhanced this technique. We prefer this pressure-sensitive web for most types of fused projects.

Thread

Along with needles and other notions, thread has played an important role in the evolution of quilting. Every quilter collects thread and has his or her favorite types for different tasks.

Thread has evolved to meet quilters' needs. In the late 1980s, Cindy taught her hand quilting students to wax thread with beeswax so it wouldn't fray when sliding through the layers. About that time, many companies started producing coated hand quilting thread so quilters no longer had to use beeswax.

When machine quilting became popular, companies had to create stronger threads that could withstand the stress of the free-motion movement. Quilters constantly made discoveries about thread by experimenting. Cindy recalled when the president of Mettler thread suggested that she try machine quilting thread in the bobbin during free-motion quilting. It worked beautifully.

Decorative silk, rayon, variegated and metallic threads created new opportunities for quilters, according to Joyce A. Drexler, executive vice president of Sulky of America.

"Contemporary quilters have discovered the same

Thread has changed to meet quilters' needs.

creative possibilities sewing enthusiasts discovered years before the first computerized embroidery machine came to market. Decorative thread is truly the sewing artisan's paint," Drexler said. "That is one of the reasons why the company introduced a decorative cotton thread line available in an array of colors, along with its Blendables™ line, which features subtle changes of hue and color for added dimension in quilting."

Superior Threads has made it a point to listen to quilters when it comes to their product base, according to Heather Purcell, company representative.

"Quilters have voiced their desire for certain qualities in their thread, such as stronger thread with less lint for machine quilting and more precise dyeing patterns for variegated thread," Purcell said. "The contemporary quilter uses thread as a design element. It is as important as the block pattern, fabric or quilting design."

When the first International Quilt Market took place three decades ago, companies primarily were selling polyester thread, remembered Ted Finkelstein, national sales manager of Gütermann of America Inc.

"Naturally, we always heard from the 'purists' that they would only sew with cotton. Interestingly though, I have noticed over the years that many quilters are 'closet' polyester thread users," Finkelstein said. "We also were surprised to see the popularity of long-arm machines grow within such a short period of time. Because of that, we had come out with larger cones of cotton thread."

Gütermann also has an extensive line of beads, which are perfect for crazy quilts and contemporary embellishments. The company's cotton hand-quilting thread is among our favorites; it is well-coated with a Glacé finish and comes in 50 gorgeous colors.

Batting

Quilts used to mostly be hand quilted and designed to cover a bed. For this, quilters wanted soft batting that draped and was easy to needle. Up until the early 1980s, polyester batting dominated the market and was the preferred batting for hand quilters and bed quilts.

But the increasing popularity of machine quilting and the creation of wall quilts brought about the need for other batting types. Firm batting was needed to help wall hangings stay flat. Quilters now can use cotton or wool batting for any project, because these fibers machine quilt beautifully.

Although Mountain Mist is the oldest batting company, its products remain on the cutting edge. The company constantly is developing new products for quilters, such as fusible, no-baste batting. Mountain Mist invented commercial filler products and has produced and marketed quilt batting, fiberfill and pillow forms for the quilting and craft trade since 1846. Their polyester batting is among our favorites for hand quilting.

As art quilts and machine-quilted pieces have expanded quilting beyond its traditional forms, functions and techniques, new batting products have evolved.

"The invention of cutting mats and rotary cutters, coupled with innovative designs from sewing machine manufacturers, fabric converters and batting companies, has made the art of quilting more accessible to busy artists," said Chuck Waimon, the chief operating officer for Fairfield Processing Corp. Fairfield manufactures cotton and polyester fiber products, including batting, fiberfill and pillow forms.

"Quilt making in America has evolved significantly since its renewed popularity during the bicentennial in the 1970s," Waimon said. "Quilting has advanced from its utilitarian uses to an art form where every means of expression is legitimate. The beauty of the very traditional, hand-quilted bed covers to the contemporary, machine-quilted art quilts inspires us to continue expanding our line to provide our quilters with the products they need to achieve the results they desire."

One of our favorite batting choices for machine quilting is Warm & Natural, which is made by The Warm Co. The manufacturer also makes our favorite fusible web, Steam-A-Seam2.

"Over the last 10 years, quilting and quilt-related items have become more mainstreamed," said Dawn Pereira, vice president of marketing for The Warm Co.

"What used to be considered grandma's hobby is embraced by young and old, men and women around the world," Pereira said. "Quilting today has been elevated to a highly regarded art form documenting our history, keeping us warm and welcoming new babies. While the styles, techniques and fabrics continue to change, one thing always remains the same — the generous, kind and loving heart of the quilter."

Like tools and notions, batting has evolved to meet the needs of today's quilter, according to H.D. Wilbanks, president of Hobbs Bonded Fibers.

"In 1982, Hobbs started the craft division and started to listen to the quilters," Wilbanks said. "They complained that the old battings quilted like a brick. So Hobbs developed an 80 percent/20 percent cotton-polyester batting to meet quilters' needs, he said. A trend toward faster machine quilted projects has prompted another shift in quilters' batting needs, and cotton batting now outsells polyester batting."

Fabric

One thing that most quilters have in common today is that they are "fabricholics." Quilters collect fabric and can't seem to get enough of it, especially from their favorite designers or companies.

When quilting began a major evolution in the late 1970s, fabric companies began creating fabric just for quilters. VIP and Concord designed coordinated fabric groups. Jinny Beyer was a great influence during those early days, designing some of the first signature fabric lines for RJR Fabrics.

In the 1980s, fabric designers focused on color rather than print design. As a result, quilters were limited in choice. And by the early 1990s, quilts took on a new art form: wall quilts. For the first time, quilters were accepted as fabric artists. We think of Nancy Crow, Michael James, Caryl Bryer Fallert and

Libby Lehman: Now that is art, not just quilting.

"Quilters are much more likely to think outside the box when designing a quilt," said Jason Yenter, a fabric designer, quilt maker and president of In the Beginning Fabrics. "They aren't afraid to break tradition and create their own design."

Paula Nadelstern designs fabrics for Benartex.

Quilter and author Paula Nadelstern designs fabrics for Benartex. Her second line of prints, named Symmetry, is one that she holds dear. "It stirs everything I love about colorful patterned cloth into versatile fabrics that work well with an eclectic mix of printed and dyed textiles," Nadelstern said.

Fabric choices and changes have played a key role in the evolution of contemporary quilting, according to David Locher, president of Benartex Inc.

"Many contemporary quilters either work with hand-produced fabrics or must search endlessly for just the right fabric for their particular type of quilting or project. In the past, this limited the number of quilters in the contemporary field. Now, thanks to advancements in the dye formulations and equipment, we are able to simulate hand-produced fabrics and make complicated, high-quality designs that one could never have dreamed of in the past. In fact, we recently placed one of our printed fabrics next to a hand-dyed fabric, and quilters could not tell the difference just by looking!" Locher said.

"Today's fabric prints are bigger and bolder, and they don't always come in a coordinated line," said Donna Wilder of Free Spirit, one of the new fabric companies. "Quilters need to be inspired by fabric, such as the hand dyes by Heidi Stroll Weber, which are so unique they make a statement all by themselves. In some contemporary fabrics, the 'printed line' is the beauty of the fabric; they don't fit into the standard color walls of a fabric store."

Fabric designers used to follow tight parameters, such as small floral prints, calicos, solids and minidots, according to Evie Ashworth, design director for Robert Kaufman Co. But those options have expanded greatly over the past two decades, Ashworth said.

"As with all companies of that era, we were mostly providing apparel fabrics and happened to have some cotton print groups that mistakenly fit the needs of fabric stores that had a Quilter's Corner," she said. "I'll never forget at a fabric show a buyer suggesting that we put our rayon challis designs on cotton for the quilting customer — duh!"

As quilters' skills improved and their confidence to become more adventurous and artistic grew, their appetites for unique fabrics increased, Ashworth added.

"As designers, we were then able to experiment with strong, bold colors, airbrushing and over-dyed techniques, 24-inch repeats, selvage-to-selvage repeats that were only printed properly in Asia where the printers are master screen engravers and use the finest dyes and cotton griege goods," Ashworth said. "Today, there is probably not a subject that isn't expressed or accepted on cloth. It is the renaissance of the cotton print designer and user."

Batiks are a favorite among today's quilters. That style of fabric began to get exposure from Hoffman California Fabrics in 1967-68, when Philip "Flippy" Hoffman began importing batiks to sell along with the company's existing retail fabric lines.

Brightly colored fabrics, such as these by Robert Kaufman Co., are a favorite among quilters.

When Hoffman traveled to Indonesia in 1966 for a surfing trip, he saw batik fabrics being sold by the local Indonesians. He was impressed by the fabrics' exquisite beauty. A short time later, he developed his own private plant in Bali, and his Hoffman Bali hand-painted fabrics were born. Those fabrics combine the art of batik with contemporary color and design.

While batik designs once were linked to the ancient life and art of the Indonesian people, contemporary quilters' influence has inspired designs of Alaskan animals, amazing flowers, luscious strawberries and bright cherries.

The Hoffman Bali Designs still are created with chops designed by Kathy Engle, Hoffman's art director. She creates black-and-white drawings of positive and negative images. Engle is famous for her designs of the Bali prints. In 2003, she received the Cotton Inc. Award for Design Excellence and Innovation for three of her Bali designs: grapes, sunflowers and falling leaves.

"While color and design have played a role in fabrics, so has production and presentation," said Irwin Bear, president of P&B Textiles. "About seven years ago we started to offer bolts with smaller cuts of fabric. This allowed shops to carry a wider variety of inventory in the same space."

Stan Gray, president of E.E. Schenck Co. and Maywood Studio, has seen amazing and sophisticated creativity evolve in the quilting world. Some of that creativity is showcased in the free patterns available at the company's Web site, http://www.eeschenck.com.

Alex Anderson, host of "Simply Quilts" TV show, also designs fabrics for P&B Textiles. Her design role is an example of a trend by fabric companies to seek the creative talents and name of a celebrity designer to add to a fabric line label.

"When I first entered into the fabric business over 35 years ago, there wasn't a recognizable quilting industry. Stores carried products and fabrics for apparel, not quilting," Gray said. "About 25 years ago, a quilting evolution began as consumers began to do more things with fabric. Chain stores dominated the industry in apparel fabrics, so independent stores tried to find a niche by carrying fabrics for other purposes, such as quilting. Interestingly, back then, this business was geared toward apparel sewing, and now there is little apparel sewing, but mostly quilting or creative sewing. This evolution has been slow, but definite."

Quilters' desires to design extend to creating their own fabrics with dyes or paints. Immersion dyeing, direct dyeing and Shibori dyeing all have been popular in clothing for decades. We've seen this custom-made fabric in quilts, too. A newer trend is using fabric paints. Painting is easier in general, but the color achieved is softer than the brilliant dye colors.

Jacquard Products, a fabric dye and paint company, gains inspiration from quilters to keep improving and inventing products, according to Kim Meyer, Jacquard's marketing manager.

"Imagine if you were a 22nd century archeologist who had dug up the last 100 years of quilting. Imagine your excitement in discovering a unique historical record which chronicled the signs of the times in images, trends of what products were being used and how that evolved over the years," Meyer said. "You would discover how paints improved in quality and ease of use, allowing quilting artists to create their own one-of-a-kind cloths."

"Quilters and shop owners have been driving forces behind changes in the fabric industry, said Rick Cohan, president of RJR Fabrics. "Quilters want more variety, often buying smaller amounts of a lot of different prints. So shops can carry a larger variety, we have decreased the amount of fabric on a bolt. The standard bolt size was 25 yards. From there it went down to 15 yards, and now there are often deals where the shop owner can buy a print on a 10-yard bolt. This allows the shop owner to not have so much money tied up in inventory, and it enables more bolts to fit on the shelves, allowing more selection to the consumers."

Cohan indicated that another change was the creation of project sheets or patterns to inspire quilters about how to use fabric. The company has embraced the demand for design ideas on its Web site, where it features a variety of patterns, many of which are available to quilters free of charge.

RJR Fabrics' Web site features free patterns for quilts, such as this Vineyard quilt, which is among the company's past free pattern offerings. To learn more, visit RJR's Web site at http://www.rjrfabrics.com.

Machine Quilting

One of the most fundamental changes to quilting has been the acceptance of machine quilting. With machines, quilters can finish a quilt in weeks, even days.

Manufacturers have changed their machines to meet the needs of contemporary quilters.

"Husqvarna Viking has added flatbed extension tables, longer arms to give more room for bulky projects, special feet for free-motion work, sensor-pressure feet, and quarter-inch feet or buttons to move the needle for quarter-inch seams," said Sue Hausmann, Husqvarna Viking vice president, host of "America Sews" and co-host of "America Quilts Creatively."

The company recently created a contemporary technique called bobbin work. For instructions on this technique and free patterns, visit the Web site at http://www.husqvarnaviking.com.

"Such advances are a departure from the machines that the company offered when it first began making them in 1872," Hausmann said. "During the turn of the century, it was considered prestigious to own a sewing machine, so oftentimes contrasting threads were used to show off the stitching. The machines were used primarily for utilitarian needs — sewing products out of necessity. Times have changed. Today we sew because we want to, not because we have to, making the process as enjoyable as the finished product."

Bernina of America also has changed its offerings to meet the expectations of the times, according to Gayle Hillert, vice president of Bernina of America education department.

"Over a dozen years ago, our company realized that a large number of the American sewing market was devoted to quilt making, so we developed special features on our machines for the quilters, like the patchwork and free-motion quilting feet, a straight-stitch needle plate and seam guides, and stronger motors to accommodate machine quilters," she said.

Bernina's emphasis is on people who use their sewing machines for the majority of their projects, she added. "It took a long time to gain acceptance for machine-quilted work, but machine skills are now considered valuable," Hillert said. "Quilters want precision and are very dedicated to their work."

In the early 1990s, the popularity of the long-arm quilting machine changed how some quilters viewed quilting, as they now could focus on quilt tops and have the piece quickly machine quilted. A new generation of quilters — those who make only quilt

Manufacturers have altered their machines, such as this Husqvarna Viking Designer I model used by "Contemporary Quilting" co-authors Cindy Walter (above) and Stevii Graves, to offer features geared toward contemporary quilters.

tops — has emerged. Long-arm quilting has made a real splash in our industry, and quilters who specialize in that skill can create glorious patterns that go way beyond stippling.

"Fifteen years ago, there were just a handful of these quilters," said Janie Donaldson, co-host of "Quilt Central" TV show and a long-arm quilter with more than 20 years of experience. "Quilters who specialize in long-arm techniques offer quilting line designs that have transcended beyond a simple meander to actual thread painting."

Companies such as Golden Threads have created new continuous-line stencils, pattern packs, books and pantographs to be used by quilters who employ hand, long-arm, short-arm and home quilting system techniques. Golden Threads represents designers from the United States and Australia.

"In the past, stencils were for hand quilters, and the books of patterns were for those few who used their sewing machines to quilt," said company owners Cheryl and Jim Barnes. "One of the biggest changes in recent years is the elimination of the need to mark your quilt top. We developed a quilting paper that you simply trace the design once, then needle punch, without thread, through a stack with the traced piece on top. Then you pin one of the stitchable stencils in place and quilt following the design."

Magazine Publishers

Quilters do not just collect fabrics. They also collect quilting books and magazines. The publishers of these books and magazines are too numerous to

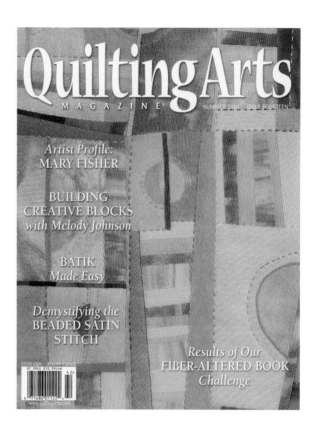

Specialty magazines provide quilters with both information and inspiration.

list, but they have all have played an important role in inspiring quilters around the world.

Most quilters know of Quilter's Newsletter Magazine, the oldest quilting magazine, which was launched in 1969. The original publication was a black-and-white mimeograph, which since has evolved into a full-color magazine.

"Our goal is to inspire thoughts about quilts, including charities, celebrating, grieving, human rights, and to make a difference in the quilting world," said Tinna Battock, publisher for Primedia, which prints Quilter's Newsletter Magazine. "The editor, Bonnie Lehman, is truly one of the founders of the modern quilt industry. The trends in the quilting world have evolved to machine usage, creativity and artistic expression."

Another one of our favorite magazines, which also is published by Primedia, is McCall's Quilting. The magazine is sleek and elegant, and it makes us proud to be quilters.

Manufacturers, quilters and creative risk-takers all have played a role in the evolution of quilt making, according to Beth Hayes, McCall's Quilting editor.

"Coming from a long line of Midwestern quilters, watching the resurgence and ultimate explosion of quilt making has been a dream," Hayes said. "Ultimately, it's quilters themselves who brought us to this remarkable place. For pure inspiration, take a stroll around the

Houston or Paducah show. My thrill is being witness to the acceptance of all forms of quilting creativity by quilters the world over."

Quilting Arts Magazine is one of the newest publications on the market. Its editor in chief, Patricia "Pokey" Bolton, said she saw a need for an art quilt and embellishing magazine, because she no longer was challenged by traditional magazines.

The quarterly publication premiered in January 2001 with 5,000 copies. Its most recent issues have had press runs of 85,000 copies. Bolton remains on the lookout for new, unknown artists and encourages people to experiment with projects and think outside the box.

New Frontiers

Quilt Shops

Advances in trends and technology wouldn't have been enough without the shop owners who were brave enough to spend the money to travel to the first quilt markets and to stretch their inventory to include new products and ideas. It would be impossible to list all of the shops around the country that contributed to this movement.

Anita Covert owns Country Stitches in East

Cindy Walter's 1997 quilt, "A Touch of Van Gogh," highlights the Snippet Sensations® technique. The quilt was featured in her book, "More Snippet Sensations."

Lansing, Mich., which is one of the largest quilt stores in the United States. Covert stocks thousands of bolts of fabrics and so many books that you could read a new one every day of the year. Her store's class schedule is mind-boggling, as it offers as many classes as a small college.

"Quilting is here to stay," Covert said. "It is my goal to provide quality products and education to quilters of all skill levels and interests, from traditional to contemporary."

We also think of Diana Leone, who founded Quilting Bee in California 30 years ago. She started by teaching quilt making at San Jose State University in 1973 and opened a quilt shop at the same time. Leone said she became an author out of necessity, because, at the time, there weren't many quilting books for the students. Several of those original books, such as "The Sampler Quilt," sold more than 1 million copies and became standard teaching manuals in shops across the United States. In 1998 this author, fabric designer and dedicated quilt maker sold her shop to her son.

Computers and the Internet

The computer also has made a huge impact in the field of quilting. Digital photography is playing an important role, not only with photos printed on special fabric, but even with fabric being created directly from photography.

Most quilters use the Internet every day, and 60 percent of quilters have high-speed connections. There are quilting chat groups of all types to lend support and inspiration. Many quilters have developed friendships over the Internet, even international friendships. And, the Internet is the main way quilters now find out about the hundreds of challenges, competitions and quilt shows around the world. If you search for the word "quilting," more than 1 million sites turn up. Many of those are for retail stores and manufacturers, who want to show the latest products, offer free patterns and give quilters inspiration.

Quilters started using computerized graphic programs to design block patterns years ago. But it never was easy, and the results weren't very professional. Now, with the help of several newer programs, designing patterns on the computer is easy for people at all skill levels.

One of our favorite quilt designing computer programs is the Electric Quilt. Company owner Penny McMorris recalled that the program originated because her husband, Dean Newmann, loved quilts and admired quilt makers. Although Newmann had no computer experience, he imagined the computer as a creative tool perfect for quilts' repeating patterns. He started his work in the late 1980s, and in about 2-½ years, he'd created the first Electric Quilt.

"This first software could be described merely as a fun toy for quilters," McMorris said. "But with each successive EQ version, we've seen our users' designs increase in sophistication and originality. For the last two years, two of the top winning quilts at the International Quilt Festival in Houston started as EQ designs. It's wonderful how much you learn from repeatedly working through your own ideas rather than replicating someone else's design. And we're convinced that today's quilters have benefited by all the technology available today."

Now that we know something about where contemporary quilters have come from, one can only imagine where they are going to go next!

The Projects

Part 2

If you haven't already done so, we'd like you to think outside the box when making your next quilt. Use the projects on the following pages only as inspiration; change them in your own unique fashion. Also, study the quilts in Part 3 The Gallery for inspiration. Remember, you are now a contemporary quilter, which simply means there are no rules or limits. Enjoy the process.

Door Quilt

This easy project is designed to teach you how to quilt a continuous free-motion line. We also show how to sew a 45-degree miter and an unusual 30-degree miter on your binding. Make this door quilt for any season.

- **Featured skill:** Continuous free-motion line quilting
- **Dimensions:** 5½" x 19½"
- **Year:** 2004
- **Designer:** Julie Mullin, Fiberactive Quilt Co.
- **Quilt made by:** Cindy Walter

Cut

From the fat quarter of blue fabric cut:
- 3 strips, 1½" x 22", for the binding
- 2 rectangles, 6" x 20", for the quilt

Draw and Trace

1. Draw a 5½" x 19½" rectangle on the quilting paper. Draw a line down the center of the rectangle. Measure 2½" from the bottom, then draw a line across the triangle. Connect the cross line on each side to the bottom center to form triangle at the bottom.

2. Center the bottom tip of the tracing paper over the bird pattern, about 1" up from the tip. Trace using a pencil or permanent pen.

3. Flip the tracing paper over. Place the top half of it on the pattern so the motifs connect. Trace the pattern on the top area.

Quilt

1. Layer the top fabric, batting and backing fabric. Place the marked tracing paper on top of the fabric sandwich. Secure all four layers with spray baste.

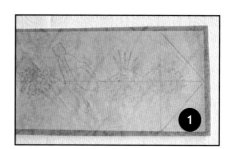

2. To free-motion machine quilt the project, put the darning foot on your sewing machine and drop the feed dogs. Place your choice of thread on the top and in the bobbin. Start at one end of the bird pattern and follow the continuous line pattern to quilt the top. For even stitches, run the machine fairly fast and move your hands slowly. Remove the project from the machine.

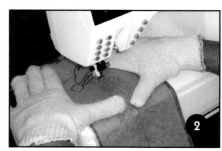

Materials, Tools and Supplies

Fat quarter of blue fabric (quilt and binding)

6" x 20" cotton batting

Package of Golden Threads Quilting Paper, 12" wide

Fine-tip permanent ink pen

Spray baste (KK2000 or 505)

Matching or contrasting thread

6" stick or wooden dowel

Thin rope

Embellishments, such as bells or beads

Tweezers (optional)

Basic quilting supplies, including pencil, scissors, rotary cutting equipment and sewing machine with regular and darning feet

3. Center the project on the cutting mat. Trim it to the 5½" x 19½" finished size and trim the off the bottom triangles to make the point. We found it easier to quilt the project before trimming it to the smaller size.

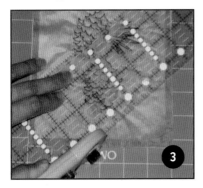

4. Remove the tracing paper by pulling lightly on the bias of the fabric until the paper tears away. We used tweezers to remove tiny pieces in the middle areas.

Finish

The Door Quilt's binding uses 45-degree miters on the top corners and bottom point and 30-degree miters on the bottom sides of the point. To make it easier, we used a single-fold binding of the same blue fabric.

1. Sew the three 1½" x 22" fabric strips together to create one long strip of binding.

2. Place the binding strip right side down on the top of the right-hand side of the quilt. Fold the starting area of the binding to form a triangle.

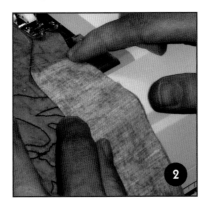

3. Sew the binding to the edge of the quilt using a ¼" seam allowance. When you reach the first corner, which will be a 30-degree angle, stop ¼" from the edge. Remove the needle from the project. A pencil dot ¼" from the new edge can serve as a sewing guide.

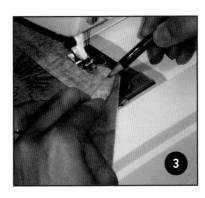

4. Rotate the project in the machine so you are ready to sew in the next direction. Fold the binding straight up.

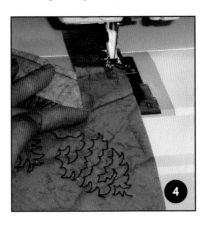

5. Fold the binding downward along the next sewing line.

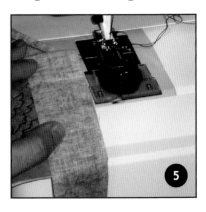

6. Starting at the edge, sew this seam. Stop ¼" from the next edge. Remove the needle from the project. A dot at the corner can serve as a stopping guide.

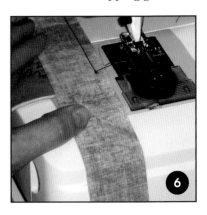

7. Rotate the project in the machine so you are ready to sew in the next direction. Fold the binding straight up.

8. Fold the binding downward along the next sewing line.

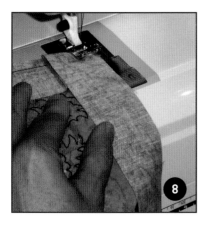

9. Starting at the edge, sew the next seam. Remember to stop a seam allowance's worth of space away when you come to a corner and to take your needle out of the project before folding your binding.

10. When you reach the end of your quilt, overlap the starting point of the binding until you cover the folded area.

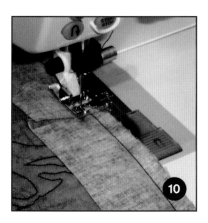

11. Work from the back to turn under the binding. Fold it under ¼", and then fold it under another ¼" onto the back of the quilt.

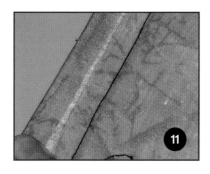

12. Slip stitch the binding to the quilt. When you come to a corner, fold the seams onto each other to create a miter.

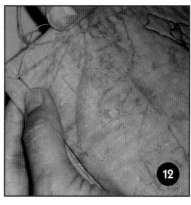

13. For the casing, fold about 1" of the quilt's top edge over onto the front of the quilt. Sew along the binding.

The gap between Julie Mullin's front door and storm door is too small to hang a wreath, so she created this darling door quilt, which measures 5½" x 19½", as an alternative for the holidays. This talented Australian artist owns the Fiberactive Quilt Company and designs patterns for all occasions. We thank Julie for her charming pattern.

Embellish

1. Slide a stick or piece of wood into the casing.

2. Attach a rope at both ends of the stick to create a loop from which to hang the quilt.

3. Attach any type of embellishment to the rope ends. We also added a bell to the very bottom point.

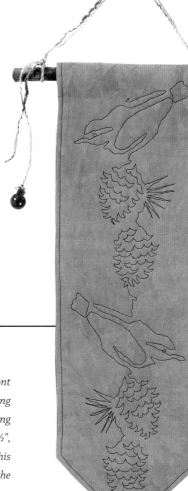

Pink Ribbon Quilt

Designer Rosie Gonzalez is the owner of Rosie's Calico Cupboard in San Diego, Calif. As a strong supporter of cancer patients, she has organized volunteers to make quilts for children's cancer camp, chemotherapy caps, mastectomy pillows and tote bags. Rosie designed this quilt for women with breast cancer. The quilt shown is the one that co-author Stevii Graves received. Stevii decided to make her quilt into a survivor's quilt by collecting signatures of breast cancer survivors on the front of the quilt. Present this quilt, with love, to someone battling breast cancer. It will make a difference. Visit Rosie's Web site at http://www.rosiescalicocupboard.com and thank her for this wonderful quilt.

- **Featured skill:** Charity project with pieced triangles
- **Dimensions:** 60" x 60"
- **Year:** 2004
- **Designer:** Rosie Gonzalez
- **Quilt made by:** Charity group at Rosie's Calico Cupboard

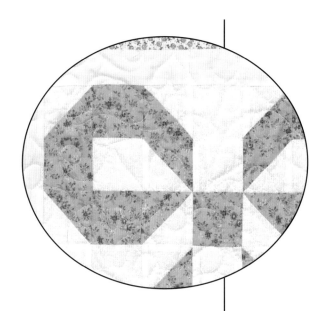

Cut

Place the white and pink fabrics right sides together and cut:

- 81 squares, 2⅞" x 2⅞"; keep the pieces sandwiched together.

From the white fabric cut:

- 180 squares, 2½" x 2½"
- 28 strips, 2" x 14½"
- 18 strips, 2" x 17½"

From the pink fabric cut:

- 99 squares, 2½" x 2½"

From the sashing fabric cut:

- 24 strips, 2¼" x 17½"

From the cornerstone fabric cut:

- 16 squares, 2½" x 2½"

From the border fabric cut:

- 8 strips, 4½" x 42"

From the backing fabric cut:

- 1 square, 62" x 62"

Materials, Tools and Supplies

2⅓ yd. white fabric (blocks)

1 yd. pink fabric (blocks)

¼ yd. medium pink fabric (cornerstones)

1½ yd. pink fabric (sashing)

1⅛ yd. dark pink fabric (border)

4 yd. fabric, 62" wide (backing)

⅝ yd. fabric (binding)

62" x 62" batting

Matching or contrasting thread

Basic quilting supplies, including pencil, scissors, rotary cutting equipment and sewing machine

* We simplified the directions for this quilt by using one pink fabric. To get the scrappier look of the quilt that is shown, use various pink fabrics.

Sew

1. To prepare the half-square triangle units, draw a light pencil line diagonally on the wrong side of each of the 81 white squares of fabric that are sandwiched with the pink fabrics.

2. Sew a ¼" seam on each side of the pencil line.

3. Cut the squares diagonally on the pencil line. This will create 162 half-square triangle units.

4. Sew the half-square triangles and white and pink squares together to create nine blocks; follow the block diagram below. Iron toward the darker fabric.

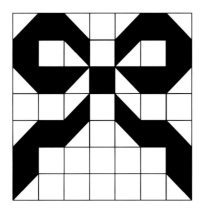

5. Sew a 14½" white strip to the sides of each block. Then sew a 17½" strip to the top and bottom of each block. Refer to the block photo at right.

6. Add sashing strips to the blocks by sewing a strip to the left-hand side of all of the blocks in the top row. Sew the sashed blocks together to create the top row.

7. Sew one sashing strip to the right-hand side to finish the row. Press the seam allowance toward the sashing strips. Repeat this for all of the rows.

8. Create the cornerstone rows by sewing a cornerstone square to the left-hand side of three sashing strips. Sew the cornerstone units together to create a strip.

9. Sew a cornerstone square to the right-hand side of the strip to finish the cornerstone row.

10. Create four cornerstone rows. Press the seam allowance toward the sashing strips.

11. Sew the block rows together, placing a cornerstone strip in between each row. Sew a cornerstone strip to the top and bottom to complete the sashings.

12. Press the seam allowance toward the cornerstone strips. Sew two border strips together to create a long border. Repeat three times.

14. Sew borders to each side of the quilt, and then to the top and the bottom.

Finish

1. Layer the finished quilt top, batting and backing fabrics.

2. Hand or machine quilt the piece as desired.

3. Bind the quilt as desired.

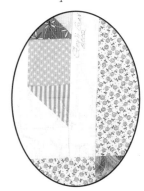

Mr. Bear's Feet

This quilt uses the traditional Bear Paw pattern, but it is modernized with the rubber stamping in the sashing. The quilt is named for Irwin Bear, owner of P&B Textiles, whose company created the fabric used in this quilt. Rubber stamping is a great way to personalize a project.

- **Featured skill:** Stamping
- **Dimensions:** 35" x 43½"
- **Year:** 2004
- **Layout designed by:** Stevii Graves
- **Quilt made by:** Stevii Graves

Cut

With the background and claw fabrics placed right sides together cut:

- 96 squares, 1⅞" x 1⅞ (Keep squares sandwiched together for the half-square triangle units.)

From the claw fabric cut:

- 12 squares, 1½" x 1½"

From the background fabric cut:

- 48 strips, 1½" x 4½"
- 48 squares, 1½" x 1½"
- 10 cornerstones, 2" x 2"

From the paw pad fabric cut:

- 48 squares, 3½" x 3½"

From the sashing fabric cut:

- 31 strips, 2" x 7½"
- 10 squares, 2" x 2"

From the background fabric cut:

- 4 inner strips, 1" x 42", which are ironed in half lengthwise, wrong sides together

From the border fabric cut:

- 4 strips, 4½" x 44"

From the backing fabric cut

- 1 rectangle, 37" x 45"

Materials, Tools and Supplies

1 yd. fabric (background)

½ yd. fabric (paw pads)

⅓ yd. fabric (claws)

½ yd. fabric (sashing)

⅝ yd. fabric (borders)

1⅓ yd. fabric (backing)

⅓ yd. fabric (binding)

37" x 45" batting

Rubber stamp

Ink stamp pad for fabric

Basic quilting supplies, including pencil, scissors, rotary cutting equipment, cutting mat, sewing machine, ironing board and iron

We simplified the directions by using one fabric for the paw blocks. You can use scrap fabrics for a different look.

Sew

1. Draw a light pencil line diagonally on the wrong side of each of the 96 background squares of fabric that are sandwiched with the paw fabrics.

2. Sew a ¼" seam on each side of the pencil line. Cut the sewn squares diagonally on the pencil line. This will create 192 half-square triangle units.

3. Sew the half-square triangles, background squares and paw pads together; see the block example. Sew 12 blocks. Iron the seams toward the darker fabric.

4. Add sashing strips to the blocks by sewing a strip to the left-hand side of all of the blocks in the top row. Sew the sashed blocks together to create the top row. Sew one sashing strip to the right-hand side to finish the row. Press the seam allowance toward the sashing strips. Repeat for the remaining rows.

5. Create the cornerstone rows by sewing a cornerstone square to the left-hand side of three sashing strips. Half of the cornerstones are from the background fabric and half are from the sashing fabric. Follow the photo on Page 25 for placement. Sew the cornerstone units together to create a strip. Sew a cornerstone square to the right-hand side of the strip to finish the cornerstone row.

6. Create five cornerstone rows. Press the seam allowance toward the sashing strips.

7. Sew the block rows together with a cornerstone row between each row. Sew a cornerstone strip to the top and bottom to complete the sashings. Press the seam allowance toward the cornerstone strips.

8. Sew an inner border strip to each of the quilt's two longer sides, with the folded edges toward the center of the quilt. Repeat for the remaining sides.

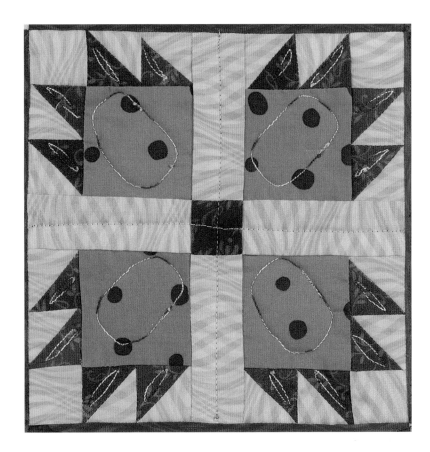

9. Sew one outer border strip to each of the quilt's two longer sides. Then sew one border strip to each of the remaining sides. Iron the narrow strip toward the center.

Embellish

1. Stamp the ink bear paw design on the sashing strips. We used a rubber stamp by Coronado Island Stamping.

2. Set the ink according to the manufacturer's directions. We used an iron set on "cotton" for 15 seconds in each area.

Finish

1. Layer the finished quilt top, the batting and the backing.

2. Hand or machine quilt the piece as desired. We used quilting techniques that accentuate the paw features.

3. Bind the quilt as desired.

Nishikigoi Pond

Martha Nordstrand is an award-winning appliqué artist who uses a computer on which to draw her original designs, including the one for this quilt. She then printed the design on sticky-backed label paper. This contemporary technique is accurate and makes the small pieces easy to handle. Her love of nature, especially flowers, is expressed in her quilts.

- **Featured skill:** Applique using a contemporary technique
- **Dimensions:** 13" x 34"
- **Year:** 2004
- **Designer:** Martha Nordstrand
- **Quilt Maker:** Martha Nordstrand

Materials, Tools and Supplies

½ yd. of dark blue water fabric (background)

7" x 13" piece of light blue sky fabric (background)

2" x 13" piece of medium blue fabric (background)

Assorted scraps of orange, yellow and tan fabrics (fish)

Assorted scraps of green and pink fabrics (flowers and leaves)

½ yd. fabric (backing)

⅓ yd. fabric (binding)

Batting, 15" x 36"

Sheet of sticky-back label paper

Card stock for viewing window

Small, flat-edge screwdriver

Glue stick

Fabric basting glue

Plastic page protector

Paper and fabric scissors

Fine-point black permanent fabric marker

Thread

Perle cotton No. 3 in medium green

Embroidery floss in yellow, medium green

Light box (optional)

Basic quilting supplies, including pencil, ruler, ironing board and iron

Cut

From the blue water background fabric cut:

• 1 rectangle, 13" x 27"

From the backing fabric, cut:

• 1 rectangle, 15" x 34"

Assemble

1. Sew the light blue fabric to the medium blue fabric along the 13" edges. Sew the dark blue fabric to the medium blue fabric.

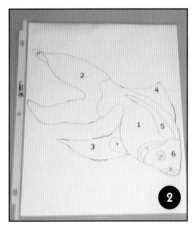

2. Photocopy or trace the four appliqué patterns that are at the end of this project onto a piece of paper. Assign a number to each appliqué pattern piece. Place the copy in a page protector; it is your master pattern.

3. Trace the pattern pieces onto a piece of card stock and onto a sheet of label paper. Use a light box, or tape the pattern and paper to a day-lit window. Transfer the numbering system to the traced pattern pieces. Leave at least ¼" between the pattern pieces. Note on the pattern pieces if a portion of the piece is under a neighboring piece by placing X's along that edge. The card stock will be a viewing window; the label paper will be the template.

4. Cut out the label paper pattern pieces on the pattern line. Leave the card stock edge intact; cut out the patterns to create windows.

5. Use the patterns printed at the end of this project to cut out:
• 2 sets of fish
• 1 set of reversed fish (Martha used a copy machine to boost the size of her fish pattern by 10 percent.
• 16 flower petals from various pinks
• 8 leaf pieces from green fabric
• 7 grass pieces

6. Create 45" of ¼" wide green bias tape for lily flower stems by cutting ¾" strips from the green fabric on the bias of the fabric.

7. With the wrong side of the green bias strip fabric facing up, iron a ¼" seam allowance toward the center on both sides of the strip. The raw edges will meet in the center of the strip.

8. Turn the green bias strip over. Use basting glue to attach it to the foundation on the quilt. Hand appliqué in place.

9. Choose the fabric for the fish and flowers by moving the window template around on the fabric to find a section of fabric that gives the desired effect for that motif. When you find the right place, remove the backing on the corresponding label pattern, and place it inside the window on the fabric. Remove the window. You have successfully captured the area of the fabric you want for that pattern piece.

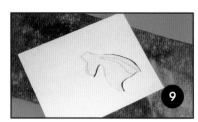

10. Leaving at least ⅛" seam allowance, cut the fabric out around the pattern. Carefully clip around curves or inverted curves. Allow ¼" seam allowance on the edges marked with a row of X's. Leave the label pattern on the top of the fabric.

11. Use glue stick to baste under the edges of each pattern piece, which is placed label-face down.

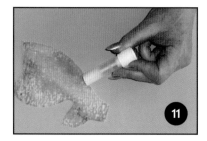

12. Turn the edges over toward the back of the fabric using the flat edge of the screwdriver. Ease around corners and curves. The glue will grab the fabric and make a crisp edge. The label edge serves as a guide for how much seam allowance to turn under. Remember to check the front of each pattern for any rows of X's first so you avoid accidentally gluing those edges under.

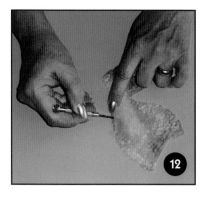

13. Set the pieces aside for 5 minutes to allow the glue to set. Remove the label; the piece now is ready to appliqué to the base. Each label can be used four to five times.

14. Arrange groupings of the appliqué pieces on the master template until the pieces are in position. Use basting glue to anchor each piece in place on the grouping and to the other pieces.

15. Once the glue is set, peel the entire grouping off the template and place it on the background fabric as shown in the photograph of the quilt.

16. Secure the grouping with basting glue.

17. Appliqué by hand or by machine. Rinse the piece thoroughly in warm water until free of residual glue. Air-dry and block in shape.

Embellish

1. Use green perle cotton to fern stitch seaweeds onto the quilt.

2. Use six strands of yellow embroidery floss to create French knots to embellish the flowers.

3. Use a permanent black fabric marker to draw the fish eyes.

4. Add embellishments. Martha Nordstrand, who created this quilt, embroidered details in the leaves with an outline stitch using one strand of embroidery floss.

Finish

1. Layer the finished quilt top, batting and backing.

2. Hand or machine quilt the piece as desired. Martha hand quilted this quilt with random wavy line to indicate water movement and wind in the sky section.

3. Bind the quilt as desired.

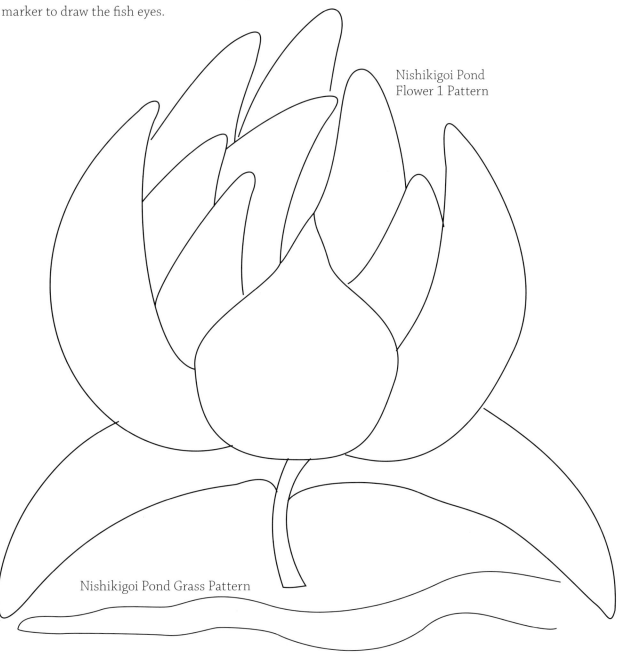

Nishikigoi Pond
Flower 1 Pattern

Nishikigoi Pond Grass Pattern

Nishikigoi Pond
Fish Pattern

Nishikigoi Pond
Flower 2 Pattern

Log Cabin with a Message

A photo transfer technique was used to create fabric for this special story quilt. Every year at the Point Bonita Retreat in the San Francisco area, Judi Warren Blaydon, Yachi Monarrez and Stevii Graves challenge one another using a single Log Cabin block as a starting point. Stevii was delighted when the challenge was a memory quilt because the design was already in her head. The quilt abstractly tells a story with words and pictures about the love and camaraderie shared by Judi, Yachi and Stevii, and all of the women who attend this retreat every January. This technique can be used to tell any story.

- **Featured skill:**
  Traditional pattern with a contemporary twist: photo and word transfer

- **Dimensions:** 18" x 20"

- **Year:** 2004

- **Designer:** Stevii Graves

- **Quilt maker:** Stevii Graves

Cut

From the backing fabric cut:
- 1 rectangle, 20" x 22.

Assemble

1. Collect photos of a special place or event. We used 10 photos. If they are digital pictures, manipulate them to fill the computer screen . If they are traditional camera snapshot prints, fill the bed of a color copier with them.

2. Type in words that support the theme of the story. Use an easy-to-read font in sufficiently large point size, such as 20. List the words in a column; be sure to leave ample space between words to allow for seam allowances.

3. Place the special fabric sheets in the printer or color copier. Follow the manufacturer's directions for use of the fabric sheets.

4. Print the photos and words. After the fabric sheets have cured, pull the stabilizing paper off of the back of the sheets.

5. Paint the word list with transparent fabric paint to coordinate with the photos. Paint also can be added to a photo to enhance its color or to alter the photo.

6. Using rotary equipment, cut the photos and word sheets into lengthwise strips that range in width from 1½" to 2½".

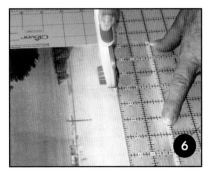

Materials, Tools and Supplies

Digital photos and a computer with color printer, or regular photos and color copy machine

Cotton fabric sheets for inkjet printers (such as Jacquard's Print on Cotton, Printed Treasures by Milliken, Colorfast by June Tailor or Quick Fuse Inkjet Fabric™ Sheets by June Tailor), or cotton fabric and Bubble Jet set concentrate.

⅔ yd. fabric (backing)

20" x 22" batting

Coordinating or contrasting thread

1 small bottle of blue transparent fabric paint (We used Cerulean Blue Dye-Na-Flow by Jacquard.)

Small drop cloth

Various inexpensive foam brushes

Basic quilting supplies, including pencil, scissors, rotary cutting equipment, sewing machine, ironing board and iron

7. Start with a 2" x 3" center piece from any of the photo strips. Add a strip first to the bottom of the center, then add strips clockwise around the quilt.

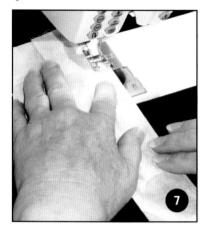

8. After sewing on each strip, iron the seam allowance away from the center of the block, then square up the block. If a strip is too short, simply add another piece to it, even if it is on the diagonal.

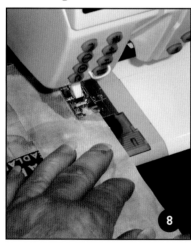

9. View the progress of the project on a design wall to help determine which strip should come next. Continue to add strips until the project size reaches 18" x 20".

Point Bonita

Log Cabi

Challen

Finish

Prepare the completed quilt top for quilting. This method lets you sandwich the project without having to bind it at the end.

I. Place the backing fabric on the quilt top, right sides together. Place the batting on top of the backing fabric.

2. With the quilt top as the top layer, sew around the edge of the quilt, using a ¼" seam allowance. Leave an 8" opening on one side of the quilt.

3. Turn the quilt right side out. Press it flat.

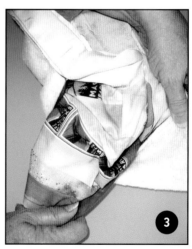

4. To close the quilt sandwich, topstitch ⅛" along the edge of the quilt, catching the 8" opening.

5. Hand or machine quilt the piece.

Part 2 The Projects

Random Rectangles

This quilt is an exercise in freedom. Sew blocks together, then trim them to create rows, which you then sew back together. We embellished the base with layers of contrasting colors, fiber lace and Angelina hair. The pink and green fabrics were designed for Hoffman Fabrics of California by Kathy Engle. Feel free to change any of the dimensions as you create, but remember to recalculate batting and backing measurements.

- **Featured skill:** Free-piecing, fiber lace, Angelina hair, embellishment collage

- **Dimensions:** 46" x 49"

- **Year:** 2004

- **Designer:** Cindy Walter

- **Quilt maker:** Cindy Walter

Cut

From the pink fabric cut :

- 1 rectangles, 13" x 16" (Column 1)*
- 1 rectangle, 13" x 15" (Column 1)*
- 1 rectangle, 9" x 20" (Column 2)*
- 1 rectangle, 13" x 14" (Column 3)*
- 1 rectangle, 13" x 16" (Column 3)*

From the green fabric cut:

- 1 rectangle, 13" x 12" (Column 1)*
- 1 rectangle, 9" x 11" (Column 2)*
- 1 rectangle, 9" x 12" piece (Column 2)*
- 1 rectangle, 13" x 13" (Column 3)*

*The column width is the first number in the dimensions

From the fat quarters, cut:

- Various-sized rectangles; ours were 4" x 6" to 6" x 8"

Assemble

1. Sew the 13" wide pieces together for Column 1. Alternate colors, placing pink on the top and bottom and green in the middle.

2. Sew the 9" wide pieces together for Column 2. Alternate colors, placing green on the top and bottom and pink in the middle.

3. Sew the 13" pieces together to form Column 3. Alternate colors, placing pink on the top and bottom and green in the middle.

4. Sew the three columns together.

Materials, Tools and Supplies

1 yd. pink fabric (rectangles)

1 yd. green fabric (rectangles)

4 fat quarters in contrasting pinks and greens (rectangles)

1 yd. fabric (outer border)

½ yd. fabric (inner border)

¼ yd. fabric (binding)

Approximately 50" x 50" batting

1 yd. fusible web (We used Lite Steam-A-Seam2 or Steam-A-Seam2)

Spray baste, KK2000 or 505

Neutral sewing thread

Basic quilting supplies, including pencil, scissors, rotary cutting equipment, sewing machine, ironing board and iron

Scrap bag of threads and yarns*

1 package Sulky Ultra Sulvy dissolvable stabilizer*

1 package Angelina Hot-Fix Fibers*

Paper towel*

Butcher paper, wax paper or Teflon sheet*

Optional materials for fiber lace and Angelina embellishment

5. Attach a piece of fusible web on the wrong side of each of the extra fabric rectangles. Re-trim the rectangles and fusible web together.

6. Pull the second liner of the web off the back of each fabric rectangle. Randomly place the rectangles on the quilt top. We layered several colors. Have fun, move them around and reposition these fun embellishments until you are happy with the results. Set the areas with the web; use a hot steam iron and iron in place for 15 seconds in each area.

7. Add borders to the quilt. Measure the longest side of the pieced top. From the inner border fabric, cut two strips that are 2" wide by the desired length. We did not precut borders for this quilt because of the freedom to change the dimensions in the piecing process.

8. Sew the strips onto the pieced top. Iron toward the borders.

9. Measure the remaining sides. Cut two strips that are 2" wide by the desired width.

10. Sew the strips on the remaining sides. Iron toward the border.

11. Repeat Steps 7 through 10 for the outer border, cutting it at least 6" wide.

Embellish (optional)

Fiber Lace

1. Collect threads, scraps of yarn and even tiny pieces of fabric.

2. Place a 12" x 12" piece of dissolvable stabilizer onto your work surface. Spray it with spray baste. Sprinkle the stabilizer with the scraps until it is covered.

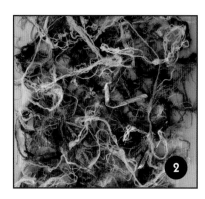

3. Spray the scraps with spray baste. Add a layer of dissolvable stabilizer on top.

4. Use a regular foot on the sewing machine to sew grid lines ½" apart on the sandwich of fibers.

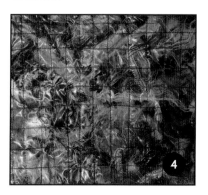

5. Take the finished grid to the sink and rinse away the stabilizer. Let it dry flat.

6. Cut the dry piece into several random-shaped pieces, and place them around your quilt. Spray baste the embellishments in place on the quilt.

Angelina Hair

Angelina hair is made from polyester fibers, which permanently bond to one other with the heat of an iron. If your you can't find this item at your local shop, check the Web site where we found it: http://www. thesilkworks.com, or call (757) 424-5893.

1. Sprinkle a small amount of Angelina hair on a paper towel, parchment paper or Teflon ironing sheet. We used the leftover release papers from the fusible web.

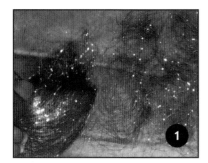

2. Place another piece of paper on top of the hair. Iron the paper-topped unit for about 5 seconds with a warm iron on a low setting.

3. Remove the top paper. Peel the fibers off the paper. Place them around your quilt, and spray baste them in place.

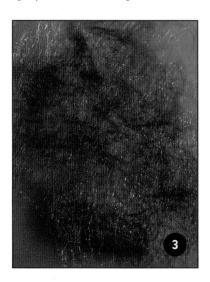

Finish

1. Create a piece of backing fabric large enough for the project. Cut a piece of batting the same size.

2. Sandwich the quilt top with batting and backing.

3. Machine quilt the piece using a free-motion design of your choice. Be sure to catch the edges of the fiber lace and the Angelina hair to secure them.

4. Bind the finished quilt as desired.

Curves Collide

This quilt is fun — and easier than it looks — because you freely cut curves and sew the seams together. That's right — without a pattern! Cindy combined bright colors for a smashing effect and then couched on decorative yarns for embellishment. Make the quilt any size to suit your fancy. Remember, this is an exercise in freedom. Change any of the dimensions as you create; just remember to recalculate your border, backing and batting measurements once the curved center is finished.

- **Featured skill:** Free piecing of curves and couched yarns
- **Dimensions:** 46" x 47"
- **Year:** 2004
- **Designer:** Cindy Walter
- **Quilt maker:** Cindy Walter

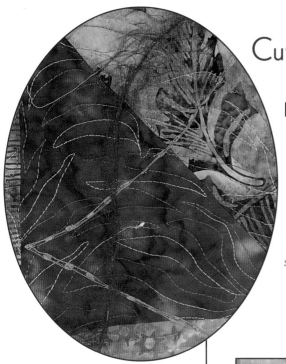

Cut and Assemble

1. Lay the first two fat quarters or scraps of fabric on the cutting mat, right sides up. Overlap them where you intend to place the curve. Use the rotary cutter to cut a soft, sweeping curve .

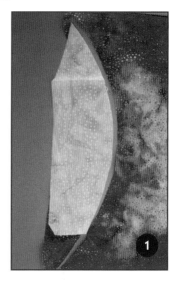

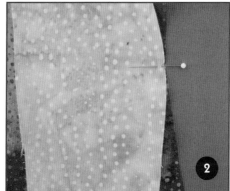

2. Place the smaller piece on top of the larger one. Pin it at the curve.

Materials, Tools and Supplies

8 fat quarters in different fabrics (quilt pieces)

1½ yd. fabric (backing)

1⅓ yd. fabric (border)

48" x 49" batting

Decorative yarns

Basic sewing and quilting supplies, including pencil, pins, scissors, rotary cutting equipment, sewing machine with regular and darning feet, ironing board and iron

3. Clip ⅛" into the inward edges.

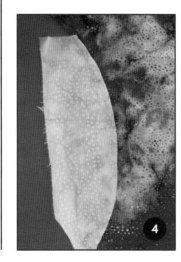

4. Use a ¼" seam allowance to sew the curved seam by easing the pieces together. Iron the seam toward the inward curve.

5. Add the next piece in the same manner. Lay the fabric right side up on the area where you want the next curved seam.

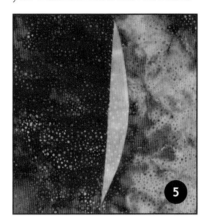

6. Cut and sew this piece just like the first one. Iron the seam.

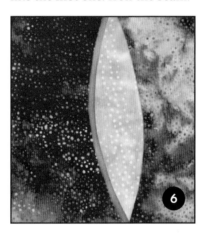

7. Add pieces, working outward, until the quilt is the desired size. Iron after each seam is sewn.

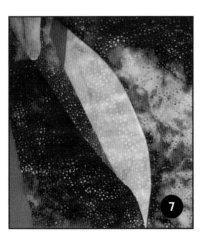

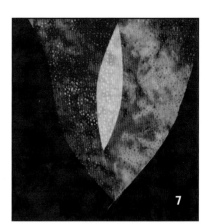

8. Use rotary equipment to trim the quilt to the desired size. Our final size was 30" x 33".

9. Measuring the longest side of the pieced top. Cut two strips of that length by the desired width for the border. Sew the strips onto the pieced top. Iron toward the border.

10. Measure the remaining sides. Cut two strips this length by the desired width. Sew the strips to the remaining sides. Iron toward the border.

Finish and Embellish

1. Hand or machine quilt the piece as desired.

2. Bind the quilt as desired.

3. Embellish. Cindy couched on decorative yarns with a light zigzag stitch. She found a straight stitch worked better on some yarns, especially eyelash.

Painted Lily

In this project, designer Cindy Walter hand painted a whole cloth for the base, then appliquéd hand-painted lilies and lily pads. Fabric painting is fun and easy. The exact paint colors used are listed, but you are encouraged to experiment with different colors of your choice.

- **Featured skill:** Fabric painting
- **Dimensions:** 33" x 30"
- **Year:** 2004
- **Designer:** Cindy Walter
- **Quilt maker:** Cindy Walter

Cut

From the backing fabric cut:

• 1 rectangle, 32" x 35"

Paint

1. Place the fat quarter base fabric on the drop cloth. Spray the fabric with water to slightly dampen it.

2. Use abstract strokes and a small foam brush to paint the base with the first color of blue.

3. Add the red, yellow and violet paints to cover the base. Allow the base to dry completely, then iron it on a hot setting to set the paint.

4. Work on a clean area of the drop cloth to create the appliqué items, lilies and pads. With a pencil, draw 20 lily petals, varying from 3" to 4" long, on the white fat quarter. For stability, we used a new product from Jacquard, which is fabric mounted on paper. Leave about ½" in between each petal. Also draw 8 abstract ovals, about 5" long, for the pads; be sure to leave ½" between each item.

5. Use a small brush to paint the petals with a base of white opaque paint. Immediately add yellow or pink paint to give the petal shading.

6. Use a small brush to paint eight 4" long oval green pads. Add a touch of other colors, even metallic paint, for shading.

7. Allow the petals and pads to completely dry. Iron to set the paint. Do not cut out the appliqué pieces yet.

Materials, Tools and Supplies

2 fat quarters of white fabric (base, lilies, lily pads)

⅛ yd. fabric (inner border)

¼ yd. fabric (outer border)

1 yd. fabric (backing)

⅓ yd. fabric (binding)

32" x 35" cotton batting

Thread

Fusible interfacing

Spray baste

2½ ounce bottle of opaque white fabric paint (We used Jacquard Textile.)

2½ ounce bottles of transparent fabric paint (We used Jacquard Dye-Na-Flow in golden yellow and magenta for petals, two greens for lily pads, and a mix of colors, such as azure blue, red, yellow and violet, for the base.)

2½ ounce bottle of purple metallic fabric paint; optional (We used Jacquard Lumiere)

Painting supplies, including 1" to 3" foam brushes, 1 fine-bristled brush, drop cloth, disposable bowls, water spray bottle, gloves and paper towels

Basic sewing and quilting supplies, including pencil, pins, scissors, rotary cutting equipment, sewing machine with regular, darning and zigzag feet, ironing board and iron

Applique

1. Use fusible interfacing to baste under the edge of each appliqué piece. To do this, place a piece of fusible interfacing on top of the petal and pad painted fabric with the fusible side down toward the painted surface. Use spray baste to secure the piece.

2. Attach a darning foot to your sewing machine. Drop the feed dogs. Sew on the pencil lines of each petal and pad.

3. Trim out the pieces; leave a ¼" seam allowance around each piece. Clip tight curves. Make a small slit in the center of the interfacing. Turn each piece inside out so the painted part is on top and the fusible part of the interfacing faces outward on the back. Turn each piece enough so the interfacing doesn't show on the front of the appliqué piece.

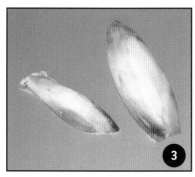

4. Follow the photograph of the finished quilt to place the pads and petals in place on the base. Iron them in place to secure the fusible interfacing.

Sew Borders

1. Choose border fabrics once the top is finished. Look for fabrics that add a nice frame.

2. Cut fabric for the borders. From the inner border fabric cut 2 strips, 2" x 21", and 2 strips, 2" x 21½". From the outer border fabric cut two strips, 5" x 23", and two strips, 5" x 30".

3. Sew the longer strips of the inner border to the longer sides of the top. Iron toward the borders. Sew the other two strips to the top. Iron toward the borders. Repeat the process for the outer borders.

Finish

1. Use spray baste to sandwich the backing, batting and top.

2. With the darning foot still on your machine and the feed dogs dropped, start quilting in the middle of the project, moving outward all the way to the edge without skipping areas. We quilted the background in swirls to represent water and quilted the lilies and pads with long, smooth lines.

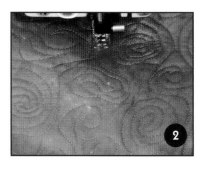

3. Raise the feed dogs. Attach a zigzag foot to the machine. Add a blanket appliqué stitch around each petal and pad to hold them securely.

4. Bind the quilt as desired.

Tropic Flowers

This quilt is a whole-cloth piece that Cindy and her family heliographed with ferns and flowers from their garden. Heliographing, also called sun printing, is an old technique to make impressions on the fabric using the sun. This technique works because when paint dries quickly, as it does under the hot sun, its pigment is dark. When it takes longer to dry, such as under objects, the pigment is lighter. We machine quilted the sun printed items, couched on decorative yarns, and added free-motion embroidered plumerias as the final touch. The sun-printed base is beautiful alone, so you can stop there. Or, play like Cindy did with this quilt.

- **Featured Skill:**
  Heliographing (also known as sun printing); couched yarns; free-motion embroidery

- **Dimensions:** 30" x 40"

- **Year:** 2004

- **Designer:** Cindy Walter

- **Quilt maker:** Cindy Walter

Materials, Tools and Supplies

1 yd. white fabric (base)

1 yd. fabric (backing)

32" x 42" batting

2½ ounce bottles of transparent fabric paint (We used Jacquard Dye-Na-Flow paint in yellow, golden yellow, magenta, red and pink)

Ferns, flowers or other flat objects for imprinting

Painting supplies, including a variety of inexpensive 1" to 3" foam brushes, water spray bottle, disposable bowls and plastic gloves

Machine quilting thread

Decorative yarns

1 package dissolvable stabilizer* (We used Ultra Sulvy)

Permanent pen*

8" embroidery hoop *

White, pink and yellow thread*

Basting spray

Basic sewing and quilting supplies, including pencil, pins, scissors, rotary cutting equipment, sewing machine with regular, darning and zigzag feet, ironing board and iron

*Optional materials for free-motion embroidery of flowers

Cut

From the white base fabric cut:
- 1 rectangle, 30" x 40"

From the backing fabric cut:
- 1 rectangle, 32" x 42"

Paint

1. Collect ferns, leaves, flowers or other flora.

2. Place the white base fabric in direct sunlight on the grass or on a drop cloth. This project works best when there is no wind.

3. Mist the fabric with water.

4. Disperse the yellow, red and pink transparent paints around the fabric with a brush until the white base is completely covered. If the paint is not blending, spray the fabric with more water. Avoid using opaque or metallic paints.

5. Immediately place the ferns, leaves and flowers on the painted fabric. Flatter objects inhibit air circulation, resulting in a better heliograph image. Cindy found the process worked better by covering some ferns and flowers with weights that did not extend outside the object they covered.

6. Allow the project to dry completely in the sun. The objects will leave a lighter image on the fabric than areas left to dry exposed directly to the sun.

7. Once the project is dry, iron with a hot iron to set the paint.

2. Attach the darning foot on your sewing machine. Drop the feed dogs. Start near the center and quilt, echoing the sun-printed images to enhance them. Rotate out, and avoid skipping areas when possible.

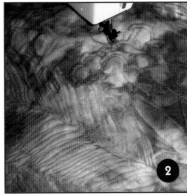

3. Once the quilting is finished, couch decorative yarns around several of the sun-printed images.

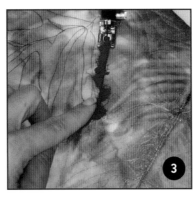

Quilt, Embellish and Finish

1. Prepare the piece for free-motion quilting by using spray baste to sandwich the backing, batting and top.

4. Create the free-motion embroidered flowers by drawing 20 petals directly onto the dissolvable stabilizer with a permanent pen. Put the dissolvable stabilizer in a small hoop, and slide it under the presser foot.

5. Starting with the white thread on the top and in the bobbin, "paint" all but 5 of the petals white with the thread. Change the thread to pink. Paint the remaining petals. Once all of the petals are white or pink, change the thread and add the yellow color.

6. Remove the dissolvable stabilizer with petals from the hoop once finished. Rinse the piece in the sink to dissolve the stabilizer.

7. Once the petals are dry, arrange them on your quilt. Baste the petals in place with spray baste, then machine stitch them in place.

8. Bind the quilt as desired.

Variation: Little Blue Sun Print

Sun printing is fun with a variety of objects and colors of paints.

Crazy Quilt

This contemporary version of a crazy quilt is the perfect project for you to use up all of those scraps that you've hoarded all of these years. Scraps cut in irregular shapes add interest to this project. Stevii also had fun using bits and pieces of leftover pieced blocks. This project utilizes the wonderful decorative stitches available on sewing machines.

- **Featured skill:** Traditional pattern with a contemporary twist and beading
- **Dimensions:** 31" x 31"
- **Year:** 2004
- **Designer:** Stevii Graves
- **Quilt maker:** Stevii Graves

Cut

From the muslin cut:
- 9 squares, 10½" x 10½"

From the border fabric cut:
- 4 border strips, 2½" x 33"

From the backing fabric cut:
- 1 square, 33" x 33"

Materials, Tools and Supplies

Approximately 2 yd. total of various random-shaped scraps of fabric (blocks)

Leftover blocks or pieces of blocks (optional)

1 yd. muslin (block foundation)

1 yd. fabric (backing)

½ yd. fabric (border and binding)

33" x 33" cotton or wool batting

Glue stick

Decorative threads

Machine embroidery needles

Spray baste

Sulky Puffy Foam (optional)

Beads and charms (optional)

Basic sewing and quilting supplies, including pencil, pins, scissors, rotary cutting equipment, sewing machine with decorative stitches, walking and open-toe embroidery feet for sewing machine, ironing board, pressing cloth and iron

Assemble

1. Start the layout of your first block either in the middle or on one corner. Place a random-shaped piece on the muslin foundation.

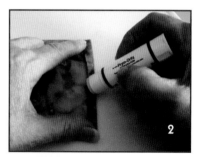

2. Lay a second piece of fabric next to the first piece. Once you like the placement, iron under a ¼" seam allowance along the overlapping edge. Let the piece cool. Run a line of glue in the seam allowance, then place it on the first piece.

3. Carefully lift the second piece. Trim the first piece so the seam allowances are even.

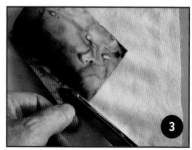

4. Continue to add pieces to the muslin in the same manner until the foundation is covered with random-shaped scraps of fabric. Occasionally add part of a pieced block as one of the fabric pieces. Iron the block to make sure it is flat.

5. Use a variety of stitches and threads to embellish the seam lines of each piece with decorative stitches or embroidery. Use a 90/14 embroidery needle and an open-toe embroidery foot on your sewing machine.

6. If desired, add dimension to some of the embroidery motifs with Puffy Foam, such as was done for the bug in the top row center block. Simply spray baste it to the fabric before embroidering. Once the embroidery is finished, tear away the excess foam.

7. Gently rinse the basting glue out of the block. Lay the block flat to dry.

8. Once the block is dry, use a pressing cloth to iron it again. Never iron over Puffy Foam.

9. Repeat Steps 1 through 8 to construct eight more blocks.

10. Trim all blocks to 9½" square.

11. Sew the blocks together in a three-block-by-three-block grid. Press the seams to one side.

12. Apply border strips to all sides; use a ¼" seam allowance.

Finish and Embellish

1. Layer the finished top, batting and backing.

2. Put a walking foot on your sewing machine. Quilt around all of the blocks before adding other quilting.

3. Bind the quilt as desired.

4. Embellish the quilt with beads, charms and other treasures, if desired.

Variation: Travel Pocket

Linda Visnaw is a Viking educator who designed this charming crazy patch travel pocket using her Designer I machine and Viking Card 130. Her project was the inspiration for the crazy quilt that Stevii Graves made.

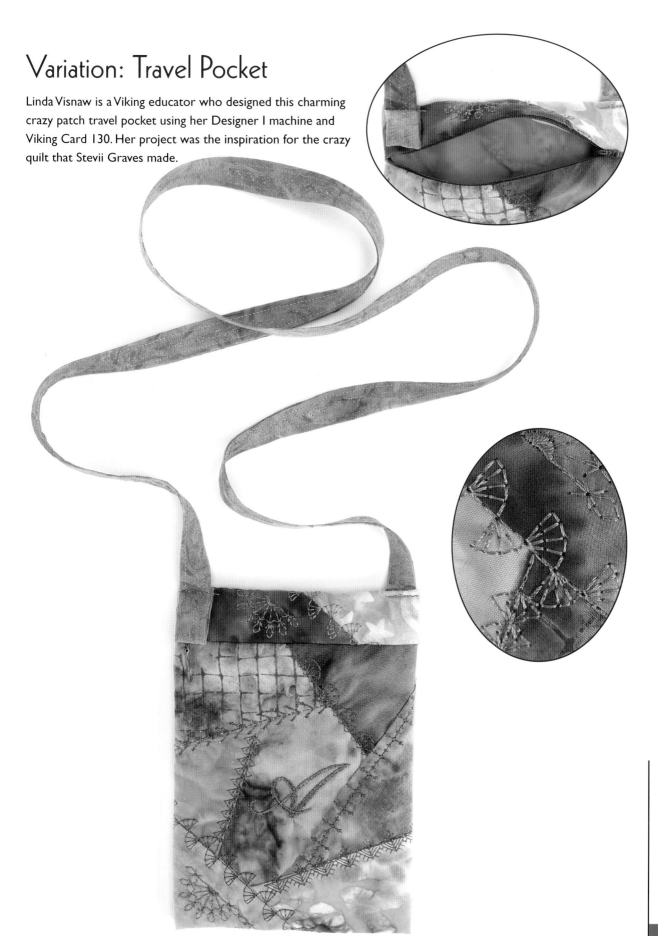

Linda Visnaw, 2004

Brittany

Snippet Sensations is a contemporary technique in which fusible web is applied to the back of the fabric before freely cutting "snippets" of fabric to create a pictorial wall hanging. This free-form technique works without measuring or drawing a pattern. In this project, Cindy first hand-painted a sunset for the foundation. You can skip this step and just use a beautiful sky fabric instead. For the snippet area, use scraps from your scrap bag; mix and match the colors. Cindy made this quilt for her friends at the French magazine Magic Patch.

- **Featured skill:** Snippet Sensations
- **Dimensions:** 34" × 30"
- **Year:** 2003
- **Designer:** Cindy Walter
- **Quilt maker:** Cindy Walter

Materials, Tools and Supplies

18" x 22" white cotton fabric or sky-colored fabric (background)

Eight 4" x 6" different-colored scraps (boats)

Six 4" x 6" blue and purple scraps (water)

Two 4" x 6" green fabric scraps (trees)

6" x 8" white fabric scrap (buildings)

6" x 8" silver fabric scrap (buildings)

⅛ yd. fabric (inner border)

⅛ yd. fabric (middle border)

¼ yd. fabric (outer border)

1 yd. fabric (backing)

⅓ yd. fabric (binding)

32" x 36" cotton batting

1 yd. fusible web (we used Steam-A-Seam2)

2½ ounce bottles of Jacquard Dye-Na-Flow fabric paint in white, periwinkle, violet, pink and yellow (unnecessary if using sky-colored fabric)

Painting supplies, including several 1" to 3" foam brushes, drop cloth, disposable bowls, water spray bottle and gloves (unnecessary if using sky-colored fabric)

Basic sewing and quilting supplies, including pencil, pins, scissors, rotary cutting equipment, sewing machine, ironing board and iron

Cut

From the backing fabric cut:

• 1 rectangle, 32" x 36"

Paint (optional)

For a no-paint project, use sky-colored fabric, and skip to the instructions under Create Snippets.

1. Place the white fabric on a drop cloth on the table. Spray the fabric with water.

2. Starting with the ocean area, paint streaks of periwinkle and violet. Leave small streaks of blank areas to add the pink and yellow reflections.

3. To create the sky, paint a thin layer of white paint over most of the sky area as a base. Add periwinkle, violet, pink and yellow streaks.

4. Let the fabric dry completely. Iron the dry fabric with a hot iron to set the paint.

5. Cindy also painted the white and silver fabrics for the buildings and boats, since regular white fabric shadows and silver fabric is hard to find. Place the white fabrics on a clean area of the drop cloth. Paint one with full-strength silver Lumiere and one with white Textile paint. Allow the fabric to completely dry, then iron it with a hot iron to set the paint.

Create Snippets

I. Collect the "palette" fabric for the snippet area. Remove one of the paper liners from the fusible web, and place the backside of the fabric to the web.

2. Trim each piece of fabric. If the web doesn't stick to the fabric, it is because some manufacturers add softeners to the fabric, which acts as an anti-cling agent. If that happens, warm the web onto the back of the fabric by ironing for about 2 seconds. Protect the iron and ironing board by placing a piece of paper between the exposed web and iron and another piece of paper between the web and ironing board.

3. Place the foundation fabric on your work table. When creating Snippet quilts, always cut the objects that are farthest away first. For this picture, that will be the trees in the background, since the sky already is finished.

4. Pull the back paper liner off of a piece of green fabric. Hold the fabric over the foundation. With the scissors right down on the foundation, use the tip of the scissors to freely cut a chunk of fabric. Cut random-shaped pieces of the different green fabrics until the tree area is completed.

5. From the silver and white fabrics, cut trapezoidal shapes for the buildings. Decorate buildings with darker-fabric windows and doors.

6. Once the trees and buildings are done, create the boats in the harbor by cutting small wedges for the tiny background boats. The boats that are farthest away are smaller and appear duller.

7. Cut large boats for the foreground. Decorate them with colorful stripes. Use the white fabric for the masts and wires. For the final touch, cut tiny slits of each boat color to create reflections in the water.

8. Use a hot steam iron to press the entire project for 15 seconds in each area. Turn the project over, and iron the back well. This will permanently set the snippets.

Create Borders

I. Choose border fabrics after the pictorial snippet top is finished. The border should add a nice frame, not distract.

2. From the inner border fabric cut two strips, 1" x 22", and 2 strips, 1" x 19".

3. From the middle border fabric cut 2 strips, 1½" x 23", and 2 strips, 1½" x 21".

4. From the outer border fabric cut 2 strips, 5" x 25", and 2 strips, 5" x 30".

5. Start with the inner border. Sew the longer strips to the longer sides of the top. Iron toward the borders.

6. Sew the other two strips to the top. Iron toward the borders.

7. Repeat the process in Steps 5 and 6 to add middle and outer borders.

Finish

1. Use spray baste to sandwich the quilt top, batting and backing layers.

2. Because of the fusible web and paint that was used, we find it best to machine quilt this project. Put a darning foot on the sewing machine and drop the feed dogs. Machine quilt with free lines that outline the objects or represent motion.

3. Bind the quilt as desired.

Postcards

This wall hanging quilt is a perfect way to document special events or vacations. It uses special photo-transfer fabric to permanently capture your images in a whimsical, collaged fashion. You can use digital photos and a color printer, or make color copies of regular print photographs. Anything goes with this type of quilt; finish it with your choice of borders, quilting or embellishments.

- **Featured skill:** Photo transfer, collage and stamping
- **Dimensions:** 32" x 40"
- **Year:** 2004
- **Designer:** Cindy Walter
- **Quilt maker:** Cindy Walter

Materials, Tools and Supplies

½ yd. black fabric (background)

1 yd. fabric (border)

1 yd. fabric (backing)

1 yd. batting

1 yd. fusible web
(we used Lite Steam-A-Seam2®)

Cotton photo transfer sheets for inkjet printers, such as Print on Cotton by Jacquard, Printed Treasures by Milliken, or Colorfast and Quick Fuse Inkjet Fabric™ by June Tailor; or, plain cotton fabric can be used with Bubble Jet Set concentrate.

Digital photos and computer with color printer, or regular photos and color copy machine

Pearl-Ex powdered pigments by Jacquard* (optional)

Stencil* (optional)

Foil Glue by Jones Tones* (optional)

Basic sewing and quilting supplies, including pencil, pins, scissors, rotary cutting equipment, sewing machine, ironing board and iron

*If your local shop doesn't carry these items, visit the Web site http://www.thesilkworks.com or call (757) 424-5893.

Cut

From the background fabric cut:

• 1 rectangle, 18" x 26"

From the border fabric cut:

• 2 strips, 8" x 28"
• 2 strips, 8" x 32"

From the backing fabric cut:

• 1 rectangle, 34" x 40"

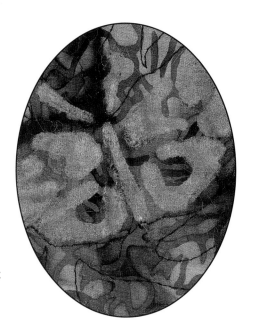

Assemble

1. Print or copy the desired photographs onto the photo transfer fabric sheets. Follow the manufacturer's directions.

2. Once the fabric sheets dry, remove the stabilizing paper backing so you are left with a piece of fabric that has photographs printed on it. Leave the fabric sheets intact.

3. Attach the fusible web to the back of the photo sheets by gently pulling off one of the release papers from the web. Be careful, because the web is fragile and can rip easily. Place the photograph fabric on top of the exposed web; gently smooth it in place. Leave the web's second release paper in place.

4. Use rotary cutting equipment to cut out each photo. The photographs do not need to be a uniform size.

Embellish

1. Add any embellishments as desired. Butterflies seemed like the perfect embellishment for this quilt since they reminded Cindy of her trip in the Alps. She placed a plastic stencil on the border area and used a small brush to apply Foil Glue in the stencil openings.

2. With a clean brush, apply Pearl-Ex on top of the glue. Let it dry for several hours. This process is fast and permanent, and it is a perfect way to add any embellishment motif to fit the theme of your quilt.

5. Lay out the black background fabric. Remove the web's second release paper from the back of each photo, and position the photos on the background. We scattered them as if they were photos pinned to a bulletin board.

6. Press the photos in place. Use a hot steam iron to press for 10 seconds in each area. Test the first photo to ensure that it does not scorch.

7. Add borders to the quilt top in any fashion you desire.

Finish

1. Sandwich the quilt top, batting and backing.

2. Hand or machine quilt the piece as desired.

3. Bind the quilt as desired.

Variation: Postcard Quilt

As another example of the postcard quilt, Stevii made this quilt with photos taken by John F. Kennedy and Z Kripe during activities of the Papillon Picnic Club of San Diego. The background first was quilted. The pictures then were appliquéd to the quilted background. She bordered her postcards with white rickrack to give them the look of deckled-edge, old-fashioned photographs.

Stevii Graves, Walking With Papillons, 30" x 40", 2004.

Stevii Graves, Postcard, 4¾" x 7¼", 2004.

Variation: Postcard

For a fast, fun project, try a single-postcard piece. Stevii added rickrack, a quick message, an inked postmark and a real stamp for a whimsical touch.

The Gallery

Part 3

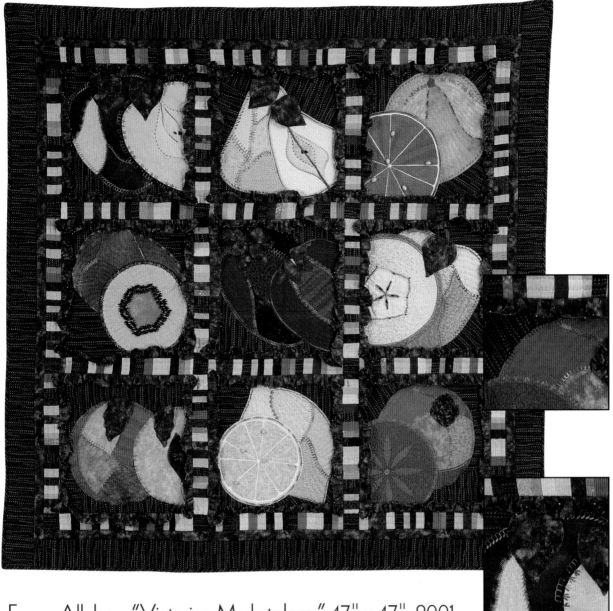

Emma Allebes, "Victorian Marketplace," 47" x 47", 2001.

Emma Allebes noticed these artful designs when slicing fruit for a fruit salad. It is machine pieced, hand appliquéd, hand embroidered and beaded. It was hand quilted by Gwen Broderick. "Victorian Marketplace" has won several awards, including a Blue Ribbon, Judges Choice, Best of Show and Viewers Choice. "When quilters were first breaking away from traditional techniques, they were creating designs that were bizarre, sad or even violent. Now contemporary quilt themes seem to be more beautiful, thought provoking, and whimsical. My personal choice is to create colorful and happy quilts that bring a smile to the viewer's face," Emma said.

Photography by Karen Bell.

Esterita "Teri" Austin, "The Well," 78" x 48", 2001.

Esterita Austin's inspiration for the design came from the ruins of abbeys, priories and cathedrals in Scotland. The way the light illuminated the centuries-old stone, casting depth and richness, captivated the artist on a trip there in 2000. Esterita also is inspired by natural objects, like the rock formations and canyons of the Southwest. She added her own new twist to using fusible web with freezer paper. She paints on top of the piece to add dimension and uses a variety of fabrics, such as velvets and satins, to add texture. This quilt won a ribbon in the Quilted Construction: The Spirit of Design competition, American Folk Art Museum, New York City. "With the invention of the rotary cutter, self-healing mats, fusibles, and Saral® transfer paper, a whole new world was opened to me: instant gratification," Esterita said. "I finally had the freedom to express myself and develop my own style. With these tools, I can't think of an idea that can't be brought to life."

Photography by Elizabeth Barton.

Elizabeth Barton, "City of Garlic and Sapphires," 58" x 57", 2002.

Viewing a city from a church tower gives it a flat perspective and lends medieval overtones. Elizabeth Barton used several techniques to dye the fabric, including shibori, immersion and screen printing. It then was pieced, appliquéd and machine quilted. "There are more people with formal art training making quilts, and this is leading to an explosion of wonderful work with much better composition with a richer color palette," she said.

Photography by Alan Benchoam.

Priscilla Bianchi, "Ceremony in Patzun," 45" x 51", 2003.

The ceremonial headdress for brides in Patzun, Guatemala, inspired this Guatemalan quilt artist to make this design. The pre-Hispanic "paya" headdress brims with symbolism to protect the newlyweds' good fortune. Priscilla Bianchi is known for using ethnic fabrics from around the world in her quilts. The weaves and colors of the fabrics lend texture and an attractive design. Her quilts, which incorporate her Mayan roots, have hung at many prestigious shows in the United States. "One art — many cultures. I think it is important to make variations or adaptations that reflect one's own identity within one's own culture. As an example in my case, my quilts reflect my heritage. I started close to traditional patterns, designs and techniques, but influenced by my roots, quickly moved into an art form that is more my own, more my culture. When you see my quilts, you see my beautiful Guatemala," Priscilla said. The piece was quilted by Laura Lee Fritz.

Melissa Bishop, "Shimmer Bay," 48½" x 68½", 2004.

This is Melissa Bishop's second quilt in a series that features architectural elements, such as a door, arches and stairs. It is constructed with a raw-edge appliqué technique inspired by Esterita Austin. The quilt showcases a variety of fabric types, has painted details and is machine quilted.

Photography by Karen Bower, Shoot for the Moon.

Judi Warren Blaydon, "The Mountain and the Magic: Haiku Moon," 84" x 73", 1993.

Judi Warren Blaydon was inspired to make this quilt by this Japanese haiku: "Under a soft moon I sought a good gate and I found one." The techniques used include machine piecing, hand appliqué, hand quilting and cloth knot embellishments that symbolize Omikuji, or fortunes written on slips of paper and sold in temples and shrines all over Japan. This quilt has been featured in several venues, including Quilts Japan magazine and the exhibitions Mementos, Memories and Meditations with Nancy Craso and Judi Warren Blaydon and Judi Warren: Quilts from the Collection of the Arts.

Photographed by Andrew Sikorski.

Jenny Bowker, "Ammonite Fault," 238cm x 180cm, 2001.

Jenny Bowker's inspiration for "Ammonite Fault" came from the way the earth traps its history in its crust with fossils and other archaeological evidence. It is from her earth skin series. The techniques used include hand-dyeing fabrics, layering, reverse appliqué and surface treatment with acrylic paints. The quilt was featured in the exhibition Twisted, which toured her home country of Australia, as well as New Zealand and Europe. In the private collection of Karen Fail.

Photographed by Dan Tilton, Photographic Solutions, Billings, Mont.

Laura Cater-Woods, "Winter Whispers 2©," 32" x 22", 2002.

Laura Cater-Woods' inspiration for this piece came from a morning walk on a river in frosty January, from which she recalls the rasping sound of breaking ice. The techniques include appliqué, free-motion embroidery, free-motion quilting and hand beading. This piece has hung at several exhibits, including the International Quilt Association show in Houston.

Hollis Chatelain, "The Grandfather," 54" x 44", 2000.

In 1992, Hollis Chatelain's family went to a New Year's celebration in Mali, Africa. The party took place on the sandy banks of the Niger River in straw and bamboo shelters in order to protect everyone from the sun. About 200 people celebrated the New Year with music, dance, good food and a lot of laughter. Chatelain photographed this grandfather, who was accompanied by his granddaughter. The grandfather was so loving and gentle that Hollis photographed him several times while he was peeling an orange for the little girl. Hollis used fiber-reactive dyes painted onto cotton fabric to recreate the portrait. The quilt then was machine quilted. "The Grandfather" was the featured art quilt in the Bernina Portrait of the Artist 2002 advertising campaign, and it has been in Quilter's Newsletter Magazine and Magic Patch magazine. In the private collection of Gwendolyn Lillis.

Sharyn Craig, "My Dad's Life," 70" x 70", 1996.

Canon Computer Systems commissioned Sharyn Craig to make this quilt completely from computer-generated fabric and photo images. She designed the quilt in honor of her father's 74th birthday to tell the story of his life. Nine photos showcase moments from his life, starting with his baptism in 1922 and ending with his career as a mechanical engineer in the oil industry. All of the fabric was generated via computer. She also imported public domain images into Photoshop® software and printed approximately 500 images, which then were cut into patches and pieced together. The quilt was featured in an article in American Quilter magazine in 1997. "The evolution of quilt making over the past 20 years has been extraordinary," Sharyn said. "Back then it was all about following a pattern; now we are encouraged to break out of those boundaries to venture beyond the existing block format and discover the incredible feeling that comes from playing with fabric in a way that no one has before."

Photography by Karen Bell.

Judy B. Dales, "Lyric Land, Mellow Moons," 41" x 66", 2003.

Judy B. Dales continuously is drawing pictures, and her favorite ones end up as quilts. This striking quilt is machine-pieced, hand appliquéd, then machine quilted. "The explorations into new materials and techniques has been astounding, but the acceptance of machine techniques (piecing, appliqué and quilting) has had the most impact," Judy said. "A quilt no longer has to be made by hand to be authentic!"

Mickey Depre, "Marmalade," 42" x 49", 2002.

Mickey Depre combined her love of geometry, gardening and quilting to craft this exquisite quilt. It combines her hand-dyed and painted fabrics along with commercial fabrics, and it features her own unique machine appliqué method. It won the prestigious award of Best Machine Quilting award and 1st place ribbon at Vermont Quilt Festival 2003, and it was shown in the Gallery showcase at the Illinois Artisan in Chicago in 2004. "I feel the biggest impact on the evolution of contemporary quilts is the acceptance that they are pieces of art," Mickey said. "Thus the use of nontraditional materials and techniques are applauded and explored without hesitancy."

Photography by David Caras.

Sandra Townsend Donabed, "Lotus Eaters,"
38" x 36", 2003.

A collection of vintage tablecloths and old embroideries inspired Sandra Townsend Donabed
to make this quilt using hand appliqué and quilting techniques. She loves giving a few
more years of visibility to these precious everyday linens and embroideries. "I love seeing
so many new people quilting, and hopefully, they will all get the same deep satisfaction I
have for decades," Sandra said. "However, as much as I love trying new techniques and art
experiments, I prefer pure fabric and stitchery over gimmicks and shock techniques."

Judy Dunlap, "View From Cougar Ridge," 51" x 44", 2003.

The wildflowers on Judy Dunlap's ranch on the central coast of California and the largest of the big cats inspired this new quilter to make this challenging wall hanging. She placed the appliquéd cat and leaves on a traditional Log Cabin background. Machine quilted by Joy Pickell.

Photography by Walter Eckmeier.

Karen Eckmeier, "Citrus Jungle," 28" x 34", 2002.

Karen Eckmeier enjoys playing with positive and negative spaces to create rhythmic patterns. Her logo is a lizard, so you'll usually find a few of them hiding in her quilts. In this quilt, she incorporated gorgeous hand-painted fabrics, curved piecing using freezer-paper templates, machine appliqué and machine quilting. Eckmeier is best known for her Accidental Landscapes. Her quilts have been featured in several books and magazines and won first place at A World of Quilts XXIII, 2002.

Photography by Mellisa Karlin Mahoney, courtesy of Quilter's Newsletter Magazine.

Cynthia England, "Open Season," 87" x 80", 2000.

A photograph inspired Cynthia England to produce this quilt using her own technique of picture piecing. This lovely quilt has been featured in several books including her book, "Picture Piecing – Creating Dramatic Pictorial Quilts." It has won many awards, including Best of Show at International Quilt Association, Houston 2000, Quilt Odyssey 2002, Indiana Heritage Quilt Show 2002, Oklahoma City Winter Quilt Show 2002 and Dallas Quilt Show 2003. "Contemporary quilting has evolved due to the availability of materials and the changing needs of the quilters," Cynthia said. "In the past, quilts were for utilitarian purposes. Now, it is more cost effective to purchase blankets for our homes, so quilts have become a means for self-expression. The abundance of beautiful fabrics and tools, such as the rotary cutter, and the use of freezer paper make the process faster and more enjoyable."

Photography by Dan Snipes, Aliso Viego, Calif.

Grace Errea, "Life After the Storm," 49" x 51", 2003.

The word "life" in the title depicts the spring flowers, or the first signs of new life that appear after stormy weather has caused destruction. Grace Errea's quilt is machine pieced, appliquéd and embroidered. The flowers are emphasized with three-dimensional appliqué and acrylic paint in the foreground. This handsome quilt has hung at several prestigious shows.

Caryl Bryer Fallert, "Midnight Fantasy No. 6©," 59" x 48", 2003.

Caryl Bryer Fallert is internationally recognized for her award-winning art quilts, which have appeared in hundreds of national and international exhibitions, collections and publications. The design for this quilt came to her during a sleepless night while she made a series of 10 small drawings to pass the time. One of the drawings was refined to produce the design for this quilt. This is the sixth quilt in a series based on her nocturnal drawings. The final design was enlarged and drawn full-size on a 4-by-5-foot rectangular piece of freezer paper to create the templates for this quilt. This illusion was created by carefully selecting fabrics for those templates in colors that blended the hues of two curves that appear to cross. Fabrics of more than 100 different colors and patterns were used, and more than 50 distinct colors of polyester and acrylic topstitching thread were used for the quilting. It was featured in the American Quilters Society 20th Anniversary Show: 2004, Paducah, Ky. In the private collection of Suzie Phillips, Jackson, Tenn.

Alba Francesca, "Oh Balls!", 87" x 87", 2003.

Quilting has been Alba Francesca's refuge from her highly stressful profession as a film producer and director. While working on a particularly difficult and drawn-out contract negotiation, she woke up one morning knowing she had to design a quilt called "Oh Balls!" She machine appliquéd the top, which then was machine quilted by Shirley Greenhoe. "Contemporary quilts are in evolution as we try to change the perception of them from bed blankets to pieces of art," Alba said. "To accomplish this, we must learn the elements of design and execution in a fine quilt are just as important as those in other mediums, such as painting, sculpture or photography. We are still seeing the disparity in prices that quilts command compared to other art pieces and are just beginning to see progress in gallery representation of contemporary quilts." In the private collection of Mr. and Mrs. Morgan Freeman.

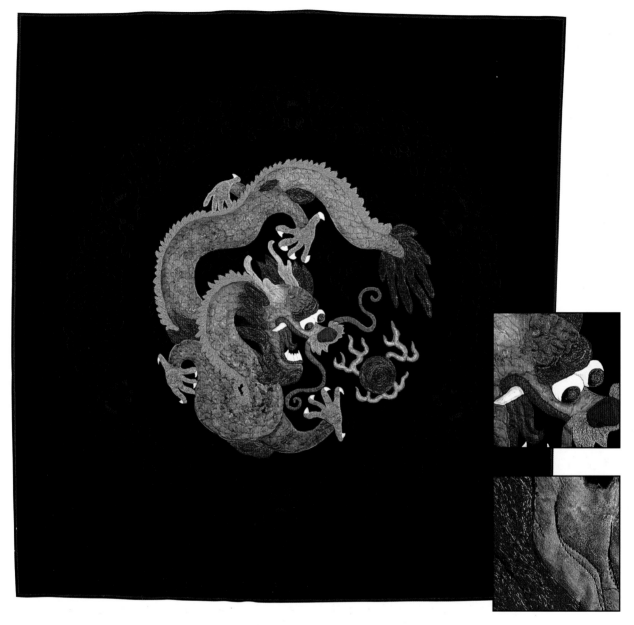

Cathy Franks, "Chasing the Pearl of Happiness," 82" x 85", 2002.

Best known for her long-arm machine quilting, you can see Cathy Franks is talented in every area of quilt making. She used a variety of techniques and materials to create her quilt, including dyeing, painting, puffy paint and thread appliqué. The thread seems to dance. This quilt has won several awards, including a prestigious 1st Place ribbon at Machine Quilters Showcase.

Charlotte Freeman, "Buck A. Roux," 36" x 79", 2004.

A small photo of a decrepit old cowboy in an article about Andy Warhol's art collection inspired Charlotte Freeman to create this cowboy. This quilt was generated by a large combination of techniques, including hand and machine appliqué, dye painting and fabric manipulation. All components of the quilt first were pinned to a muslin foundation before the appliqué began. Notice several of the pieces actually are miniature quilts, such as the saddle and belt buckle. The trapunto embroidery in several areas adds a three-dimensional effect. This impressive quilt won a 1st Place ribbon in the Innovative Wall Quilt category at Road to California 2004. "I believe long-arm quilting machines combined with the use of all the wonderful fabrics and specialty threads have had a profound impact on the evolution of contemporary quilting," Charlotte said. "My journey into the contemporary art quilt arena was ignited in a workshop with Joan Colvin. The quilt I started in that class earned me several major awards, and my quilting style changed forever as a result of that experience."

Photography by Tommy Roberts, Photo Quick.

Laura Lee Fritz, "Lady of the Universe," 56" x 61", 2003.

Laura Lee Fritz used the traditional Lady of the Lake block for this curved interpretation. She sketched a full-size pattern onto paper, which she cut up to serve as pattern pieces. It is machine pieced and long-arm machine quilted. "Thank you to the inventors of the rotary cutter and to Ken Gammill for the long-arm quilting machine," Laura Lee said. "Without these two tools, quilting would still be in the slow lane."

Stevii Graves, "My Coronado Bicycle Circa 1958," 22" x 20", 2003.

This quilt is Stevii Graves' fond remembrance of living in Coronado, Calif. In grade school, she had the freedom to ride all over the island on her bicycle. This piece was sun printed using a found object — a bicycle wheel. It is machine quilted with pebble shapes that continue to the raw outside edge.

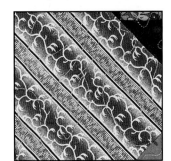

Stevii Graves, "Rebel Reveille," 54" x 54", 2004.

Stevii Graves belongs to a several small quilting groups, including The Rad Swappers, which is orchestrated by Sharyn Craig. When the group traded these traditional blocks, made with reproduction fabrics, Stevii was determined to create a contemporary block setting. Her solution was to use weeds from her back yard to create sun-printed blocks, then use these as alternative blocks in the quilt. It was important to control the paint's color so it would match the reproduction fabrics.

Mirror mirror on the wall........
Oh no! I have no hair. I look just
like Clint Eastwood's orangutan!

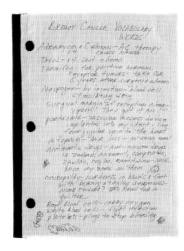

NEUROPATHY

I have Chemo Brain

What is your Excuse?

WHERE IS MY HAIR

I CAN NOT FIND

MY HAIR......

HE SAID.....UNLESS
WE JUST GOT A
CAT, YOUR HAIR IS
ON THE SOFA....

SPEED
LIMIT
55

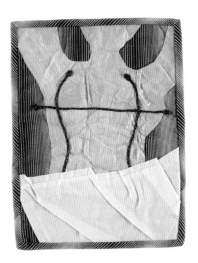

Stevii Graves, "Journal Quilt," 8½" x 11", 2003.

Stevii Graves, co-author of this book, used quilts to document her experiences during treatment for breast cancer . She used a variety of techniques to reflect her emotions and reactions to chemotherapy and surgeries. In 2002 Karey Bresenhan invited members of the online group Quiltart to make monthly 8½" x 11" journal quilts using techniques and themes of their choice to be part of a special exhibit for the International Quilt Association in Houston. Quilters also kept written journals.

Photography by Sharon Risedorph.

Cara Gulati, "3-D Party Explosion," 72" x 72", 2003.

While making a series of three-dimensional explosion quilts, Cara Gulati wanted to fashion one that looked like a flower, but which instead ended up looking like party favors. The illusion is achieved with machine appliqué and free-motion quilting. Her book, "3-D Explosion: Simply Fabulous Art Quilts" from Doodle Press, explains her technique. This quilt won the prestigious Viewer's Choice award in the International Quilt Association 2003 contest as part of the art category. "I believe contemporary quilting has taken on a whole new direction since it has become more accepted and appreciated by a wider audience," Cara said. "We aren't just sewing squares together any more or playing by the rules. The right tools speed along the process, which means I can complete my art quilts faster and have more of them to enjoy!"

Photography by Jackson Hill.

Michele Hardy, "Directions No. 16©," 53" x 41", 2003.

The notion of looking out or looking in and seeing a fragment of our world is the current theme of Michele Hardy's art. A lifelong love of geology, nature and exploration directly inspired this work and continues to supply an unlimited palette of color, texture and ideas for her. Michelle used hand-dyed, painted and screen-printed fabrics. This piece is a combination of fabric collage, machine embroidery and machine quilting. "In the past few years, we have seen an abundance of exciting products developed for fiber and quilt artists, including new threads and paints for fabric," she said.

Barbara Oliver Hartman, "Celebration in Red," 83" x 83", 2001.

This quilt is a labor of love, loss and healing. Barbara Oliver Hartman created it while mourning her mother's death, and she selected fabrics based on her mother's special love of bright colors. The quilt won the prestigious Best of Show award at the International Quilt Association show in Houston, the Pacific International Quilt Festival in Santa Clara, Calif., and the American Quilter's Society show in Paducah, Ky. "Everything has changed in the past 20 years," she said. "We have better equipment, tools, fabric choices and opportunities to show our work. Our contemporary quilts are gaining wider acceptance in the art world; the progress is exciting."

Denise Tallon Havlan, "Vanishing Warblers," 60" x 92", 2001.

This quilt maker is a figurative artist who loves costumes and makeup. Creating a geisha had been on Denise Tallon Havlan's mind for some time. All of the subjects in this piece are Japanese and endangered, except for the colorful koi. The quilt was machine and hand appliquéd, hand painted, machine embroidered and machine quilted. It has appeared in several magazines and has won several prestigious awards, including Best of Show at the Mid-Atlantic Quilt Festival, Williamsburg, Va., 2003; 2nd Place, Quilting The Quilt, Duluth, Minn., 2002; Honorable Mention, American Quilter's Society, Paducah, Ky., 2002; and 1st Place Pictorial, International Quilt Festival, Houston, 2001. "Today we are seeing more artists trained in areas of fine arts such as sculpture and painting," she said. "This has taken the art of quilting into new realms."

Photography by Helen Mitchell.

Marge Hurst, "Cosmic Flowers," 56½" x 59", 1998.

*This quilt was inspired by the flowers of spring and summer — and an invitation to make a quilt
for the 1999 Quilts in Bloom Exhibition in Germany. Marge Hurst used strip piecing techniques
with templates she developed. You often can see this famous New Zealander's quilts in the popular
New Zealand Quilter Magazine. In the private collection of Christina Porter.*

Lois Jarvis, "Ground Zero," 89" x 89", 2002.

Lois Jarvis made this quilt after Sept. 11, 2001, to pay tribute to the victims of 9-11. It reminds us that it is the people we lost who should be remembered, not the buildings or materials. She downloaded about 1,000 photos from the CNN Web site and printed 600 of them on cloth treated with Bubble Set 2000 using a Canon 600 printer. Although the design and use of photo transfer is contemporary, she mostly used traditional techniques for the piecing. The Lone Star pattern symbolizes the blast, the inner border contains the blast, and the outer gray border captures the colors of the following days. The quilt is machine pieced and machine quilted.

Melody Johnson, "No. 5 Zigzag," 52" x 54", 2003.

South African quilter Odette Tolksdorf was Melody Johnson's roommate at a New Hampshire quilt show, where both were teaching. Odette's work evoked new design ideas and feelings, which encouraged Melody to begin a series of work inspired by African motifs. Two designs in this quilt — the saw-tooth edges and Prairie Points surrounding the quilt — came from that inspiration. As one of the founders of the Chicago School of Fusing, all of Melody's work is fused. She begins by fusing her hand-dyed fabrics in half-yard widths. Then she cuts shapes from the fused fabric and overlaps the edges, leaving all of the edges unfinished. She hand quilted the top and batting together, then layered it with the backing and machine quilted all the three layers together. "Fusing allows endless possibilities for easy construction of shapes and details, which permits my creativity to flow. I no longer need to prove that I can sew a seam, make tiny hand-quilted stitches or make quilts that can be machine washed," Melody said. "Because I am a believer in fusible web, I have been able to make more quilts in less time, and therefore discover more about what is possible for me as a growing artist."

Marcia Katz, "pH Balance," 85" x 85", 1999.

Marcia Katz found motivation for this quilt in a pattern by Barbara Barber. Using black and white prints among bright colors adds movement and shows off Marcia's flair for color. Traditional patterns are being made to look contemporary — with the right choices of fabrics. This quilt has been featured in several publications and has won many awards, including Honorable Mention at the 1999 Pacific International Quilt Festival in Santa Clara, Calif.; First Place in Innovative at Road to California, 2002; and Viewer's Choice at the 2002 Glendale, Calif., show. "I love fabrics that sing and make a statement with their colors and textures," Marcia said.

Gül Laporte, "Mikado II," 70" x 70", 1999.

Well-known French quilter Gül Laporte is an author of two books, one in French and one in English. She works in several countries as a free-lance consultant in the quilting field, and she also writes articles for magazines, teaches and lectures in Europe. She loves to experiment with color, shapes and different techniques. Gül sewed square blocks randomly together, then separated them and inserted 1" strips of various reds. The quilt was machine pieced and quilted.

Photography by E.Z. Smith.

Jean Ray Laury, "urban cowgirl.com," 35" x 31", 2000.

The inspiration for Jean Ray Laury's quilt comes from the observation of the change in the status of cowgirls. Once the epitome of the independent woman, they now are into fashion, fad and style with designer clothes and makeup. The Internet brought cowgirls into full swing with city girls. Jean Ray first drew the designs and then printed them onto white cloth using Thermofax. She then silk-screened all of the patterns on each block and hand painted in certain areas. Some of the striped fabrics are commercial, but the rest are hand printed or dyed. "The biggest change in quilting is that it has become an industry. I don't feel that new tools or techniques have a whole lot of influence, it is the way we think that truly influences our work," Jean Ray said. Machine quilted by Susan Smeltzer.

Photography by Jack McConnell.

Mickey Lawler, "Sails," 58" x 47", 1992.

The paintings of Lyonel Feininger and Strauss' waltzes prompted Mickey Lawler to generate this quilt. She used hand-painted cottons with machine piecing and hand quilting. The quilt was in the 2002 Pioneers Exhibit and has the honor of being named one of the 200 best quilts of the 20th Century by the International Quilt Association. Lawler is famous for her painted fabrics. She is the author of the popular book "Skydyes," which teaches her exciting style of fabric painting. Mickey said several things come to mind when she considers the evolution of quilting. "First, the extraordinary growth in abundance and variety of beautiful fabrics available to the quilters. The second, beginning with Helen and Blanche Young's Lone Star and Trip Around the World books, is the number of wonderful minds who have devised faster and more accurate methods for constructing age-old patterns."

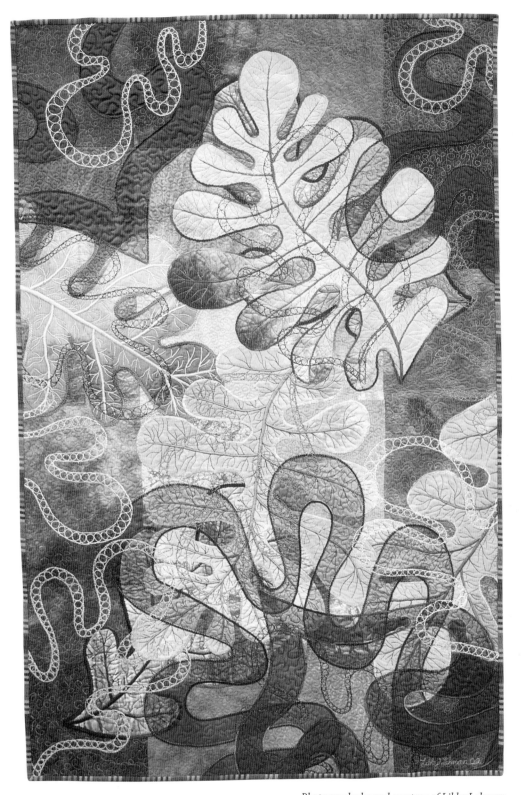

Libby Lehman, "Drift III," 30" x 46", 2002.

Libby Lehman's love of watching the fall leaves drift to earth moved her to create this lovely quilt. It is potluck appliquéd and has machine embroidery, bobbin drawing and couching of yarns. Libby is famous for the spectacular thread work on her quilts, and she is the author of "Threadplay With Libby Lehman: Mastering Machine Embroidery Techniques." This quilt appeared on the French Patchwork Magic 2003 calendar. In the private collection of Mr. and Mrs. Leroy Hardy.

Diana Leone, "Into the Light," 65" x 73", 2004.

The city of Mountain View, Calif., commissioned Diana Leone to produce this quilt. It is a memorial quilt for the late Susan Ozbuko, the city's librarian. It symbolizes the "light" that Ozbuko brought to those who knew her, as well as the light that she found at the end of her life. Many of the library staff members and patrons were customers of Diana's quilt shop, and it was a special honor for Diana to be asked to make this quilt. Drawing from nearly four decades as a fine artist, Diana hand-painted this whole-cloth quilt with a variety of paints. Machine quilted by Kim Mariani.

Jennifer Lokey, "Crown of Beauty," 39" x 39", 2003.

Jennifer Lokey has been in the quilt pattern business since 1986. Her beautiful quilt designs integrate machine embroidery. The unique contemporary appearance of this quilt comes from the machine embroidery design, which complements the alternate patchwork block.

Photography by Bread & Butter Studios, Atlanta.

Vita Marie Lovett, "Primitive Door Series No. 17 — Pete's Creek," 26" x 34", 2000.

*This quilt is part of Vita Marie Lovett's primitive door series, in which she preserves
a piece of the past — rural American barns — using fabric and thread. The design is
free-motion machine-thread painted.*

Barbara Malanowski-Casty, "The Jungle Strikes Back," 57" x 72", 2004.

This quilter from Switzerland is enthralled by the image of the jungle conquering asphalt. As plant life overtakes the man-made brick and mortar of walls and houses, nature reclaims its territory: The jungle strikes back. The top was freely cut and pieced, and then paints and other embellishments were added. This quilt was part of Barbara Malanowski-Casty's solo exhibition at Quiltfestival Höri 2004 in Germany. "We should honor tradition and learn from the ancient designs," she said. "But now, due to technology and new materials, we are able to create whatever we can imagine."

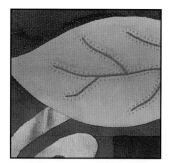

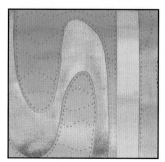

Suzanne Marshall, "A Midsummer's Dream," 17" x 72", 2001.

A line drawing attributed to Carl Schmidt-Helmbrechts in a Dover publication inspired this talented quilt maker and author to produce this quilt. This is an art nouveau adaptation reminiscent of a hot, sultry night in America's Midwest. Suzanne Marshall used hand-dyed fabrics by Artfabric with hand appliqué, hand embroidery and hand quilting. The quilt has won several awards.

Judy Mathieson, "Marbled Stars," 47" x 52", 2000.

Judy Mathieson is an author and artistic quilt maker. This quilt is a continuation of her series of stars and circling geese that use Cosmati designs based on Italian floor tiles. It is machine pieced using freezer paper foundation without sewing through the paper, and machine quilted. The quilt was a Quilter's Newsletter Workshop Sample in September 2000.

Photography by David Caras.

Ruth McDowell, "Nasturtiums 3©," 30" x 42", 2003.

Most of Ruth McDowell's ideas for her art quilts come from her abiding love of nature. This creative artist starts each of these quilts with an intense exploration of the natural subject matter before deciding which aspects uncover the spirit and should be selected for the quilt image. This project is from her ongoing series of botanical quilts. It is machine pieced and quilted using cotton fabric, threads and batting.

Barbara Barrick McKie, "Dahlias a la Mode," 26" x 31", 2003.

Barbara Barrick McKie's inspiration for this quilt came from dahlias growing in her garden. She loves to recreate flowers and textures. She created it with disperse dye and computer imagery on polyester and hand-dyed cottons. It is machine appliquéd and quilted. "I have been stretching the applications of transfer imagery in my quilts since 1994 because of my background in computers prior to re-entering the quilting world," she said. "I find people using many of the technical innovations that have happened during this period of time. I also find that artists from fields other than fiber art are finding the great textures that can be achieved with art quilting to be compelling. The 'art' has improved in the field as a result."

Kathie Miller, "Staying Alert," 44" x 33", 2003.

As a painter, Kathie Miller wanted to combine painting techniques with quilting. The red background serves as a perfect foundation to highlight the bold black and white zebra. Using the Snippet technique, she first applied fusible web and then cut the pieces in various shapes. This impressive quilt won a 2nd place ribbon at Road to California, 2004.

Margaret Miller, "Coral Ribbons," 57" x 57", 2004.

This quilt is from Margaret's Angle Play™ series and is cut using her Angle Play™ templates, which take the guesswork out of how to align triangles. It features four versions of a single quilt block, each more complex than the last. The blocks are offset from each other in such a way that the coral ribbons reach across the block lines, camouflaging where one block stops and the next one begins. "Technology has played a key role in the evolution of quilting," she said. "The rotary cutter and the blending of computer technology with sewing machines have brought the most profound changes in our industry. Computers are pervasive; it won't be long before a laptop will be on the supply list for workshops involving quilt design. Also, I have been heartened by the diminishing of prejudice against machine-quilted quilts and against the category entitled 'contemporary' quilts. Today, the word 'contemporary', when used with the word 'quilt', no longer necessarily means bizarre or hard to understand. Rather, it refers to evidence that the quilt maker has taken a step or two beyond traditional boundaries to express her own sense of design." Machine quilted by Wanda Rains of Rainy Day Quilts in Kingston, Wash.

Photography by Bewley Shaylor.

Jan Mullen, "Country Housez," 53" x 73½", 2000.

*Australian author and pattern designer Jan Mullen was inspired to make this quilt by the
production of the first fabric line she designed for Marcus Brothers. Her style is to use bright
colors, as they are invigorating and make her happy. This quilt is machine pieced and quilted.
"This quilt is different because it was made just for me — a rare thing," Jan said.*

Photography by Karen Bell.

Paula Nadelstern, "Kaleidoscopic XXII: Ice Crystals," 41" x 54", 2000.

Contemporary quilters find their inspiration in many sources. In Paula Nadelstern's case, every snow crystal that gently floats to earth is equally compelling. Our curiosity is aroused by this pure gem of nature, with its common hexagonal pattern and endless variety of structural details. The pieced snowflakes in this quilt are her attempt to translate to fabric a few of the 6,000 photomicrographs made in the late 1800s by W.A. Bentley of Jericho, Vt., and published in 1931 by the American Meteorological Society. Paula is a talented quilter, author and fabric designer. Her quilts have won many ribbons and been featured in numerous publications.

Miriam Nathan-Roberts, "A Celebration of the Hand©," 62" x 70", 2002.

A terrible fall in 2001 left Miriam Nathan-Roberts with a shattered wrist. After two painful surgeries, a bone graft and the addition of an interior metal plate and external metal apparatus whose bars went into bone, her doctors said it was impossible to predict how much function would return to her hand. That threatened a major part of her life: quilting, fabric dyeing and printing. This quilt celebrates that she regained the full use of her hand. The central panel is layered images, with the background evoking the enlarged interior of a bone. The wooden mannequin hand and medical illustration of hand bones are superimposed. Uppermost is a photograph that shows the external fixator on her arm. The border is mostly hand-printed, dyed or discharged fabric. The diamonds refer to the tradition of quilting, and they are layered with tracings of her hand.

Velda Newman, "Hollyhocks," 62" x 107", 2001.

This talented artist and author combined hand-dyed silk and cotton sateen, then added paint and pencil work. Velda Newman's works usually are hand appliquéd and hand quilted. For many years we have admired her extraordinary quilts, which are easily recognized by their large scale. She has won numerous awards for her quilts.

Martha Nordstrand, "Hola Mola!," 44" x 52", 2002.

*Martha Nordstrand came up with the idea for this quilt from a trip through Central America.
She would like us all to give tribute to the art of the rain forests. Techniques include hand
appliqué and embroidery. "In the world of quilt making, old dusty rules have been discarded and
abandoned and a new diversity has emerged," Martha said. "As a family, the quilting world has
expanded into new realms of possibilities. There is room for all of us, regardless the technique.
This diversity is the magic ingredient that will move us even further forward to push the edge of
creativity."*

Barbara Olson, "First Thought," 87" x 87", 1998.

*The love of curves caused Barbara Olson to make this quilt with arcs swirling out from the
center. It is machine appliquéd, pieced and quilted. When asked who influenced her quilting
style over the years, Barbara first mentioned Nancy Crow. This beautiful quilt won the
prestigious Best of Show award at the Pennsylvania National Quilt Extravaganza. In the
private collection of Maureen Hendricks.*

Photography by Neal Collette of Media Specialties.

Jenni Paige, "Circles & Squares," 31" x 39", 1999.

Jenni Paige included a variety of commercially printed and hand-dyed fabrics in this beautiful quilt, which she constructed using her Stitch n' Fray® technique. After deciding which prints she wanted to feature for the background, she free cut the squares and circles using scissors or a rotary cutter without a ruler. The pieces were held in place with spray baste or pins, then machine stitched through all of the layers. This method offers instant gratification, and it is especially appreciated after the quilt is washed and a three dimensional texture results from the fraying.

Emily Parson, "I'm Buggin'," 51" x 50", 1996.

Making this quilt brought back memories for Emily Parson of the car her dad taught her drive and the one she drove across the country to college. It is fused appliquéd and machine quilted. This darling quilt won the Trailblazer award at Quilt National, 1997. "I think the influence of the people who dye fabric and do surface design has been extremely important," Emily said. "It has given quilters many more choices of fabrics."

Photography by Austin Prints for Publication.

Judy Coates Perez, "Tree of Life," 53" x 61", 2003.

Judy Coates Perez wanted her quilt to have the quality of multicultural folklore using symbols from nature and religion. It was important to her that the location of the biblical Eden be placed in present-day Iraq. This whole-cloth painted quilt uses Jacquard's Lumiere fabric paints and Tsukineko inks for the faces, hands and feet. It is machine-quilted and couched with gold braid. It won an impressive Honorable Mention at both International Quilt Festival in Houston, 2003, and Road to California, 2003. "I've loved witnessing the acceptance of art quilts in the mainstream quilt world," she said. "For years I didn't enter shows because quilts like mine weren't winning awards. Contemporary quilts now have equal representation. There seems to be more people joining this trend of pushing the limits and redefining the definition of a quilt."

Photography by Sue Vande Yacht.

Jeanne L. Pfister, "Fiesta," 53" x 59", 2003.

The colors and cultures of America's Southwest served as Jeanne Pfister's inspiration for this quilt. Its spontaneous design evolved from her box of fabric choices. The quilt is machine pieced, appliquéd and embellished with couched yarns, beading, trapunto and free-motion quilting. This beautiful quilt won two 2nd place ribbons at the 2003 Crazy Quilters Guild and Road to California 2004. "Unlike the bed quilts of yesteryear, contemporary quilts are works of freedom and self-expression," Jeanne said. "Following the elements of design are the only rules needed. The evolution of the contemporary quilt has helped us to recognize that all quilts, whether traditional or contemporary, are works of art."

Photography by Sharon Risedorph.

Yvonne Porcella, "Keep Both Feet on the Floor©," 54" x 77", 1990.

Yvonne Porcella found inspiration for this quilt after tearing cartilage in her knee. The quilt is machine pieced, hand appliquéd and quilted. Striking color with bold movement is often the signature of her quilts. Yvonne succeeded in giving this quilt extra movement and energy by turning the center on a diagonal and adding buttons as embellishments. The quilt has been featured in several publications, including the book "The Twentieth Century's Best American Quilts."

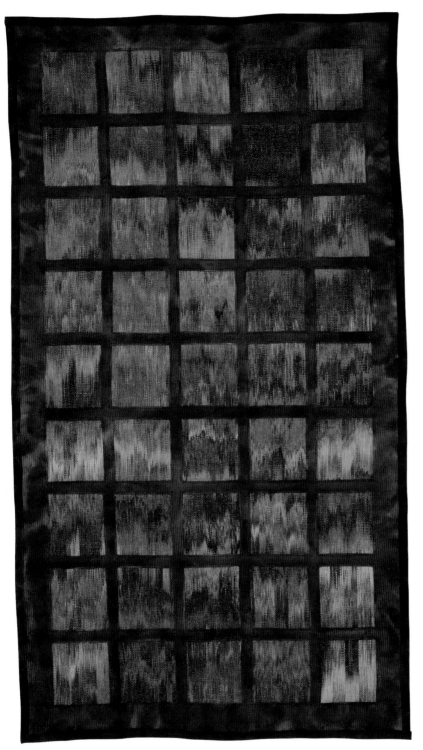

Jennifer Priestley and Bjorn Coordt, "Stained Glass Frieze," 75" x 43", 2004.

Marc Chagall's stained glass windows at a church in Metz, France, inspired this project. Jennifer Priestley and Bjorn Coordt first collected sheep and goat fleece from New England farms. Jennifer dye-painted the yarns by hand, and Bjorn, who is a famous weaver from Germany, wove them into the fabric used for the window areas. The felted wool used in the lattice also was dye-painted by hand. They enjoy working with their own handmade multifibered fabrics to create more character in their quilts.

Jan Rashid, "Ancient Pines," 38" x 46", 2004.

This quilt was inspired by the magnificent overlook at the Torrey Pines State Park in La Jolla, Calif., where the twisted shapes of the native pines cling tenaciously to the windswept bluffs over the Pacific Ocean. Jan Rashid used a combination of techniques, including machine and hand embroidery, fabric painting, stenciling, stuffed work, beading, hand appliqué and hand quilting. In the private collection of Dr. Joseph R. Rashid.

Edith Raymond, "The Phantom Takes the Lift: Maze in Black and White," 58½" x 54", 1988.

This well-known French quilt artist is a graduate from design art school who works as an illustrator, designing mainly games and cutouts. This has influenced her quilting style. Edith Raymond prefers to work in series, using first numbers, then alphabets and words, then mazes because of their graphic design and symbolism. Often masks representing the devil can be seen in the center of these mazes. This maze uses 1" strips and is machine pieced and hand quilted.

Pamela Robson, "The Muse," 14" x 14", 2003.

Pamela Robson used the computer when creating this quilt. First, she scanned a photo showing her great aunt and a childhood friend during a high school play, which was taken by Pamela's grandfather around 1916. She manipulated and enhanced the photo before printing it with an ink-jet printer. Recent advances in printing fabric via computer have given quilters a wonderful opportunity to showcase their ancestors on cloth and display them to future generations. This quilt took 2nd place as part of a trio in a mixed media competition at the San Pedro Art Association in 2003.

Photography by David Belda.

Rebecca Rohrkaste, "Floribunda," 66" x 44", 2003.

This quilt was a commissioned piece, and it is the most recent in a series of quilts using quarter circles. The quilt, which is machine pieced and quilted, won the Best Use of Color award at Pacific International Quilt Festival 2003. Rebecca Rohrkaste said she appreciates the variety of exciting hand-dyed fabrics available to quilters. In the private collection of Gay White.

Photography by Gene Schamber.

Sharon Schamber, "Our Children of Freedom," 91" x 69", 2003.

Sharon Schamber's love of children led her to create this original quilt. She used her daughter's second-grade class students as inspiration for this quilt, which is dedicated to the importance of the learning experience. It is constructed of fabrics that she hand dyed and printed. It is machine pieced and quilted. This quilt has been featured in several magazines and won a prestigious Best of Show award at the 2004 Pennsylvania National Quilt Extravaganza. "For me, the rules are gone, and I'm free to express my own ideas and designs," Sharon said.

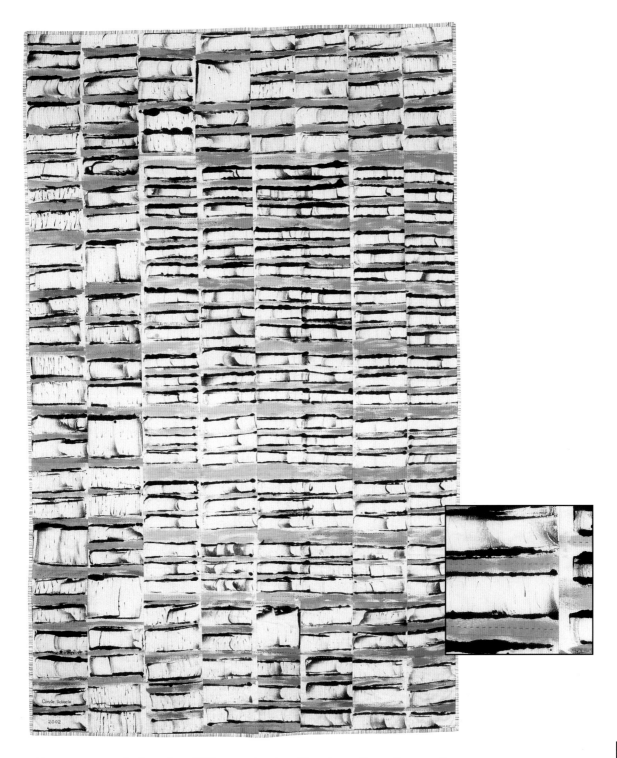

Constance Scheele, "Through the Birches," 65" x 46", 2002.

The lakes and woods of northern Wisconsin inspired Constance Scheele to make this linear composition using mono printing, machine piecing and hand quilting. This quilt won the Best of Show award at the Twisted Thread Quilt 2002 Festival of Quilts in London. It also was included in the World Wide Winners exhibit at 2003 International Quilt Festival in Houston. Her artistry emphasizes the evolution of contemporary quilting. "My work has progressed by learning more about older techniques, hand dyeing, and mono printing, and then using them in an experimental fashion," she said. "Contemporary quilts now challenge the definition of a quilt. I am eager for the day when fabric is accepted as a medium, just as paint is on canvas."

Joan Shay, "Dimensions of Summer," 72" x 72", 1998.

Joan Shay designed this quilt by combining many of her Petal Play flower designs around a Nantucket basket filled with hydrangeas. She used Appli-bond©, her three-dimensional appliqué technique, along with traditional appliqué and fabric weaving. This artist and author was featured in the Petal by Petal one-quilter show for the National Quilt Association.

Brenda Smith, "Color Blocks 2: Mardi Gras," 47" x 57", 2002.

Brenda Smith started this quilt in a workshop taught by Sandi Cummings at Road to California in 2002. She found Sandi's method of free-form cutting, slashing and piecing back together using 1" spaces to be liberating. This quilt is machine pieced and quilted with thread embellishment, and couched on yarns and ribbons. It won the 1st Place ribbon for Innovative Wall Quilt, Road to California, 2004. "Modern technology has impacted the contemporary quilt world," Brenda said. "The development of the computer, Internet and digital photography has had a tremendous impact on quilters by sharing the latest works of contemporary quilters with the world. Through this instant communication, they are sharing their knowledge and techniques, which is pushing the envelope and challenging the definition of a quilt."

Lura Schwarz Smith, "Dancing Peace©," 68" x 60", 2002.

Lura Schwarz Smith had this quilt well in progress when 9-11 hit, but she soon realized this piece actually was her statement about the catastrophic event and her hopes for the future. She believes mothers around the world all want the same thing — a world in which all children grow up in peace, with friendship and mutual respect for one another. In the quilt's center sky, the mothers reach toward a distorted Friendship Circle block. Other friendship blocks, also distorted for perspective, are pieced into the sky and stitched into each mother's garments. The fabric in this quilt is painted with textile inks, then free-form machine pieced, hand appliquéd and hand quilted with big and little stitches. The quilt won the prestigious Best of Show award at the 2002 Pacific International Quilt Festival. Lura said the rotary cutter is her favorite innovation in quilting, and it is one that lets her use a very fast, curved, paperless, machine-free piecing technique. "No matter which method you choose to work, traditionally or in the wildest stapled-together art style, there is a place for everyone's approach in today's quilt world," she said.

Trish Stuart, "Tiger Lilies," 105" x 87", 2003.

Tiger lilies remind Trish Stuart of her childhood, when her grandmother used to grow them every summer in Fairbanks, Alaska. When she later moved to Anchorage, Alaska, a close friend gave Trish some for her own garden, where the blooms drew more butterflies, dragonflies and even a hummingbird. She used crayons and inks to add some of the dimension in the appliqué in this quilt, and some ink was added after it was quilted. "The explosion of the quilting industry is partly due to the reason we need to slow down and reach inside of ourselves to express what can't be expressed with other mediums, amongst our hectic and fast-paced world," Trish said. "New fabrics and tools introduced have motivated people to realize anyone can be successful with this medium. Whether you focus on design, color, value, art quilts, traditional quilts, wall hangings, bed quilts, quilts that tell a story or any other facet of quilting, there really is something for everyone in quilting."

Deborah Sylvester, "A Woman of Color — Sari Dreams," 41" x 51", 2003.

After a long day of shopping for sari fabrics, a dream inspired this quilt by Deborah Sylvester. It is raw-edge appliquéd, partly with the Snippet Sensations© technique, machine appliquéd and quilted. Deborah is best known for creating stunning faces on her subjects. Her quilts have won several ribbons.

Photography by Carol Taylor.

Carol Taylor, "Crescendo," 67" x 86", 2002.

The exciting parts of musical arrangements often are announced in a grand forte after building in intensity from a soft pianissimo. This is called a crescendo. "Crescendo's" subtle fabric placements, which range from light to dark and are interspersed with texture, heightens its visual excitement. This quilt is part of Carol Taylor's "gong" motif series, which comes from a design of a circle representing a Chinese gong. This is the last of 39 quilts that evolved from this theme. It is constructed of hand-dyed cotton and sateen, and each piece was cut individually. This quilt won a slew of prestigious awards in 2003, including: 1st Place Large Art, International Quilt Association in Houston; 1st Place Innovative Pieced, American Quilter's Society in Paducah, Ky. and Quilters' Heritage Celebration in Lancaster, Pa.; 2nd Place, Innovative World Quilt and Textile Show in Lansing, Mich., and Manchester, N.H.; and Mid-Atlantic Quilt Fest in Williamsburg, Va. In the private collection of Mr. and Mrs. Chuck Meacham.

Photography by John Bonath, Maddog Studios, Denver.

Ricky Tims, "Bohemian Rhapsody," 88" x 88", 2002.

This quilt began as a small, original design of a paper-cut style medallion block. Ricky Tims added a border to create a small wall hanging. But this artist and author couldn't stop there. He improvised on the medallion theme, and the quilt continued to grow. It is constructed of his own original hand-dyed fabrics, machine piecing, appliqué and quilting. This quilt has won many awards, including Best of Show at Rockonic Gardens, Arcola, Ill.; 1st Place at the 2002 International Quilt Association's judged show in Houston; and 1st Place at the 2003 American Quilters Society, Paducah, Ky.

Cindy Walter, "Tranquility in Purple," 50" x 52", 2001.

Cindy Walter feels quilters should give back to their communities through their creative passions. She created this piece of wall art for a charity called Giant Steps Therapeutic Equestrian Center, a nonprofit organization dedicated to improving the quality of life of individuals with physical, emotional and developmental disabilities. The top is constructed exclusively from fabric Cindy and Jennifer Priestley hand painted when they co-authored "The Basic Guide to Dyeing & Painting Fabric." Different quilting designs embellish each block. In the private collection of Tony and Nancy Lilly.

Cindy Walter, "The Kiss II," 40" x 47", 1996.

The passion in Gustave Klimt's painting "The Kiss" inspired Cindy to create this snippet project, which was featured in her original Snippet Sensations© book. This is a great example of the fusible web snippet technique because it combines both random-shaped and predetermined-shaped snippets.

Cindy Walter, "Pathway," 46" x 56", 2004.

This quilt features rich batik fabrics, beading and fiber lace. The rectangles were randomly pieced to disperse the colors. Machine-quilted pebble shapes across the quilt designate the pathway of life. The beads are the little jewels we find along the way. This is a variation of the Random Rectangles quilt, which was featured in the project section.

Cindy Walter, "Wailele," 30" x 46", 2004.

On a sunny and calm day, Michael and Alex Lilly knew Cindy was going to heliograph several pieces of cloth. As a treat for her, they collected ferns and flowers for her to use in the sunprinting project while on a hike up the Wailele gulch on Oahu's north shore. Refer to the Tropic Flowers quilt in the project section to learn how to make a similar project. A closeup of this quilt is featured on the cover of this book.

Laura Wasilowski, "Blue Rake," 43" x 49", 1999.

As the owner of Artfabrik, Laura Wasilowski is known for her hand-dyed fabrics and as a founder of the Chicago School of Fusing. A set of hand-dyed fabrics Laura made reminded her of fall leaves and offered the inspiration for this quilt. She puts fusible web on fabrics, cuts them into any shape imaginable and quickly fuses them to other fabrics. "Fusing allows me to create improvisational artwork without limits. It is free, loose and easy," Laura said. Her quilts have appeared in numerous exhibits and publications.

Cassandra Williams, "Jigsaw Giants," 50" x 74", 2002.

Cassandra Williams specializes in animal quilts. The soft-eyed beauty and grace of the giraffe inspired her to make this quilt. It was made with raw-edge appliqué, machine piecing and quilting. "Jigsaw Giants" has won several ribbons, including Best of Innovative QPNQ 2002; 3rd Place Pictorial, International Quilt Association 2003; Viewer's Choice, World Quilt & Textile 2003; and 2nd Place Innovative, Road to California, 2004. "Contemporary quilts have vastly increased in number," Cassandra said. "Quilters have a fascination for whatever is new. For me, raw-edge appliqué has set me free to create as I see it."

Colleen Wise, "Yosemite Triptych," 46" x 40", 2003.

A family vacation to Yosemite National Park in California inspired Colleen Wise to make this quilt. She hand-dyed the fabric to recreate the play of light and shadows on the granite domes. Water droplets invite viewers to inspect the intimacy of the leaf litter underfoot. This beautiful wall hanging won Judge's Choice at the Indian Heritage Quilt Show 2003 and 1st Place Innovative Award at Road to California, 2004.

Artist Contacts

Emma Allebes
8833 Barrister Lane
Fair Oaks, CA 95628
E-mail: teemholnor@sbcglobal.net

Esterita Austin
58 John St.
Port Jefferson Station, NY 22776
E-mail: Esteritaaustin@aol.com
Web site: http://www.EsteritaAustin.com

Elizabeth Barton
Web site: http://www.elizabethbarton.com

Priscilla Bianchi
7801 NW 37th St.
Section 2903-GUA
Miami, FL 33166-6559
E-mail: pb@intelnett.com
Web site: http://www.priscillabianchi.com

Melissa Bishop
177 Lower Sheep Pasture Road
Setauket, NY 11733
E-mail: Melissa.Bisho@Stonybrook.edu
Web site: http://www.interquilt.com

Judi Warren Blaydon
555 E. Commerce
Milford, MI 48381
E-mail: Blay555@yahoo.com

Jenny Bowker
21 Brereton St. Garraw, Act, 2605 Australia
E-mail: bowker@netspeed.com.au
Web site: http://www.jennybowker.com

Laura Cater-Woods
315 Burlington Ave.
Billings, MT 59101
E-mail: Lcaterw@msn.com
Web site: http://www.artquilter.net

Hollis Chatelain
909 Lawrence Road
Hillsborough, NC 27278
E-mail: hollis@hollisart.com
Web site: http://www.hollisart.com

Bjorn Coordt
67 Tom Harvey Road
Westerly, RI 02891
E-mail: Bjorn@fabricsToDyeFor.com

Sharyn Craig
2530 Indigo Drive
El Cajon, CA 92019
E-mail: gcraig@mail.sdsu.edu
http://www.sharyncraig.com

Judy B. Dales
2254 Craftsbury Road
Greensboro, VT 05841
E-mail: jubda@aol.com
Web site: http://www.Judydales.com

Mickey Depre
4845 W. 96th Place
Oaklawn, IL 60453
E-mail: Mickey@mdquilts.com
Web site: http://www.mdquilts.com

Sandra Townsend Donabed
515 Centre St. No. 3
Newton, MA 02458
Web site: http://www.donabed.net

Judy Dunlap
Santa Maria, CA

Karen Eckmeier
19 South Road
Kent, CT 06757
E-mail: Karen@quilted-lizard.com
Web site: http://www.quilted-lizard.com

Cynthia England
803 Voyager
Houston, TX 77062
E-mail: cynengland@ghg.net
Web site: http://www.englanddesign.com

Grace Errea
Laguna Niguel, CA

Caryl Bryer Fallert
Bryerpatch Studio
P.O. Box 945
Oswego, IL 60543
Web site: http://www.bryerpatch.com

Alba Francesca
Artist's Representative: Margaret Danielak
Web site: http://www.danielakart.com

Cathy Franks
145 Maple Crest Drive
Carmel, IN 46033
E-mail: Cathyfranks@indy.rr.com

Charlotte Freeman
Wildflower Workshop
222 North Wildflower
Ridgecrest, CA 93555
E-mail: cjfreeman@mchsi.com

Laura Lee Fritz
P.O. Box 1170
Palmer, AK 99645
E-mail: houndhollr@aol.com
Web site: http://www.houndhollr.com

Stevii Graves
6529 Divine St.
McLean, VA 92122
E-mail: stevijo@yahoo.com

Cara Gulati
P.O. Box 508
Nicasio, CA 94946
E-mail: DesignBear@aol.com
Web site: http://www.Doodlepress.com

Michele Hardy
147 Acadian Lane
Mandeville, LA 70471
E-mail: mhardy@michelehardy.com
Web site: http://www.Michelehardy.com

Barbara Oliver Hartman
122 Red Oak Lane
Flower Mound, TX 75028
E-mail: winerunner@aol.com
Web site: http://www.barbaraoliverhartman.com

Denise Tallon Havlan
9081 Del Prado Drive
Palos Hill, IL 60465
E-mail: dhavlanartquilts@aol.com

Marge Hurst
5 Donlin Road
Pukerua Bay 6010, New Zealand
E-mail: mhurst@top.net.nz

Lois Jarvis
4625 Tokay Blvd.
Madison, WI 53711
E-mail: loisjarvis@USA.net
Web site: http://www.Loisjarvisquilts.com

Melody Johnson
664 W. Main St.
Cary, IL 60013
Web site: http://www.wowmelody.com

Marcia Katz
12836 Waddell St.
Valley Village, CA 91607
E-mail: KrzyQuilt@aol.com

Gül Laporte
22 Hameau de Stang Allestrec
29940 La Foret Fouesnant, France
E-mail: Gulaporte@aol.com

Jean Ray Laury
Clovis, CA
E-mail: Laury2@csufresno.com
Web site: http://www.jeanraylaury.com

Mickey Lawler
Skydyes
P.O. Box 370116
West Hartford, CT 06137-0116
Web site: http://www.skydyes.com

Libby Lehman
7618 E. Jordan Cove
Houston, TX 77055-5053
Web site: http://www.LibbyLehman.com

Diana Leone
21700 Calero Creek Court
San Jose, CA 95120
E-mail: dianaleone@comcast.net
Web site: http://www.DianaLeone.com

Jennifer Lokey
910 Vinelrest Lane
Richardson, TX 75080
Web site: http://www.jenniferlokey.com

Vita Marie Lovett
Web site: http://www.vitamarielovett.com

Barbara Malanoski-Casty
Casa Cauma
7412 Scharans, Switzerland
E-mail: malanowski@tiscalinet.ch

Suzanne Marshall
85 Arundel Place
Clayton, MO 63105
E-mail: suzannemarshall@mindspring.com
Web site: http://www.suzannequilts.com

Judy Mathieson
1977 Green Hill Road
Sebastopol, CA 95473
Web site: http://www.JudyMathieson.com

Ruth McDowell
993 Main St.
Winchester, MA 01890
Web site: http://www.ruthbmcdowell.com

Barbara Barrick McKie
40 Bill Hill Road
Lyme, CT 06371-3501
E-mail: mckieart@adelphia.net
Web site: http://www.mckieart.com

Kathie Miller
2019 Sousa Court
Fairfield, CA 94533
E-mail: animalarts@earthlink.net
Web site: www.animal-arts.com

Margaret Miller
P. O. Box 4039
Bremerton, WA 98312
E-mail: millerquilts@aol.com
Web site: http://www.millerquilts.com

Jan Mullen
9/100 Stirling Highway
North Fremantle 6159
Western Australia
Web site: http://www.stargazey.com

Paula Nadelstern
Web site: http://www.Paulanadelstern.com

Miriam Nathan-Roberts
1351 Acton St.
Berkeley, CA 94706
E-mail: Mn222@cornell.edu

Velda E. Newman
882 Gold Flat Road
Nevada City, CA 95959
E-mail: velda@veldanewman.com
Web site: http://www.Veldanewman.com

Martha A. Nordstrand
17149 W. Laird Court
Surprise, AZ 85387
Web site: http://www.morequiltsplease.com

Barbara Olson
20 Emerald Hills
Billings, MT 59101-7230
E-mail: Barbquiltart@aol.com
Web site: http://www.BarbaraOlsonquiltart.com

Jenni Paige
P.O. Box 177
Meridian, ID 83680
Web site: http://www.iwannaquilt.com

Emily Parson
175 N. 11th Ave.
St. Charles, IL 60174
E-mail: emily@emilyquilts.com
Web site: http://www.Emilyquilts.com

Judy Coates Perez
2520 St. Andrews Drive
Glendale, CA 91206
E-mail: judypereztx@earthlink.net

Jeanne Pfister
321 E. 20th St.
Kaukauna, WI 54130
E-mail: jeannelp@new.rr.com

Jennifer Priestley
67 Tom Harvey Road
Westerly, RI 02891
E-mail: Jennifer@FabricsToDyeFor.com
Web site: http://www.FabricsToDyeFor.com

Edith Raymond
35 Boulevard Pasteur
75015 Paris, France
E-mail: edith.fr.raymond@wanadoo.fr

Pamela Robson
1912 Gebhart St.
Salina, KS 67401
E-mail: pamelasews@cox.net
Web site: http://www.anotherage.com

Rebecca Rohrkaste
E-mail: Rrohrk@aol.com

Sharon Schamber
P.O. Box 42
Jensen, UT 84035
Web site: http://www.Sharonschamber.com

Constance Scheele
15135 Kimberly Court
Houston, TX 77079-5129
E-mail: cwscheele.aol.com

Joan Shay
102 Courtney Road
Harwich, MA 02645
E-mail: joanshay@petalplay.com
Web site: http://www.petalplay.com

Lura Schwarz Smith
P.O. Box 649
Coarsegold, CA 93614
E-mail: lura@lura-art.com
Web site: http://www.lura-art.com

Trish Stuart
Twisted Threads
P.O. Box 325
Emory, TX 75440-0325
Web site: http://www.twthreads.com

Deborah Sylvester
40736 Chantaco Court
Palmdale, CA 93551
E-mail: Deborah@Sylvesterartquilt.com
Web site: http://www.sylvesterartquilt.com

Carol Taylor
234 Railroad Mills Road
Pittsford, NY 14534
Web site: http://www.caroltaylorquilts.com

Ricky Tims
P.O. Box 392
LaVeta, CO 81005
Web site: http://www.rickytims.com

Linda Visnaw
2721 Via Palma Drive
Lake Havasu City, AZ 86406
E-mail: lindavisnaw@citlink.net

Cindy Walter
P.O. Box 615
Honolulu, HI 96809-0615
E-mail: Cindyquilter@aol.com
Web site: http://www.Cindywalter.com

Laura Wasilowski
Artfabrik
324 Vincent Place
Elgin, IL 60123
Web site: http://www.artfabrik.com

Cassandra Williams
712 Colonial Drive
Grants Pass, OR 97526
E-mail: Cassandra@rascal.cc

Colleen Wise
7513 91st St. Ct. E.
Puyallup, WA 98371
E-mail: wisemaas@foxinternet.net

Recommended Reading and Viewing

Colvin, Joan, "Quilts from Nature." That Patchwork Place, 1993.

Craig, Sharyn, "Twist 'n Turn." Chitra Publications, 1996.

Craig, Sharyn, "LeMyne Stars Made Easy." Chitra Publications, 1998.

Craig, Sharyn, "Ultimate Half Log Cabin." Chitra Publications, 2001.

Craig, Sharyn, and Harriet Hargrave, "The Art of Classic Quiltmaking." C&T Publishing, 2000.

Craig, Sharyn, "Setting Solutions." C&T Publishing. 2001.

Craig, Sharyn, "Great Sets." C&T Publishing. 2004.

Crow, Nancy, "Quilts and Influences." American Quilter's Society, 1990.

Dales, Judy, "Curves in Motion." C&T Publishing. 1998.

Drexler, Joyce, "Sulky Secrets to Successful Quilting." Sulky, 2000.

Gaudynski, Diane, "Guide to Machine Quilting." C&T Publishing, 2003.

Graves, Stevii Thompson (editor), "Visions Quilt Expressions." Rutledge Hill Press, 1998.

Graves, Stevii Thompson (editor), "Visions: Layers of Excellence." C&T Publishing, 1994.

LaPorte, Gul, "Quilts from Europe." C&T Publishing, 2000.

Laury, Jean Ray, "Ho for California: Pioneer Women and Their Quilts." EP Dutton, 1992.

Laury, Jean Ray, "The Photo Transfer Handbook." C&T Publishing, 1999.

Laury, Jean Ray, "Imagery on Fabric." C&T Publishing, 1997.

Lawler, Mickey, "Skydyes." C&T Publishing, 1999.

Lehman, Libby, "Thread Play." That Patchwork Place, 1997.

Leone, Diana, "Crazy with Cotton." C&T Publishing, 1996.

Leone, Diana, "New Sampler Quilt." C&T Publishing, 1996.

Lokey, Jennifer, "Machine Embroi-dered Quilts: Creating with Colorful Stitches." Martingale and Co., 2004.

Mathieson, Judy, "Mariner's Compass Quilts: New Directions." C&T Publishing, 1996.

Marshall, Suzanne, "Take-Away Appli-que." American Quilter's Society, 1998.

McDowell, Ruth, "Piecing: Expanding the Basics." C&T Publishing, 1998.

Miller, Margaret, "Blockbuster Quilts." Martingale & Co., 1991.

Miller, Margaret, "Strips that Sizzle." Martingale & Co., 1992.

Cindy Walter, "Fragrant Memories," 44" x 33", 1998.

Miller, Margaret, "Blockbender Quilts." Martingale & Co., 1995.

Miller, Margaret, "Smashing Sets: Innovative Settings for Sampler Blocks." C&T Publishing, 1998.

Miller, Margaret, "Easy Pieces: Creative Color Play with Two Simple Blocks." C&T Publishing, 2005.

Miller, Margaret, "AnglePlay: A New Look at Triangles." C&T Publishing, 2005.

Mullen, Jan, "Cut Loose." C&T Publishing, 2001.

Mullen, Jan, "Reverse Applique With No Brakez." C&T Publishing, 2003.

Murrah, Judy, "Jacket Jazz." Martingale & Co., 1993.

Murrah, Judy, "More Jazz from Judy Murrah." Martingale & Co., 1996.

Murrah, Judy, "In the Studio with Judy Murrah." Martingale & Co., 2001.

Murrah, Judy, "Jacket Jackpot." Martingale & Co., 2003.

Nadelstern, Paula, "Kaleidoscopes & Quilts." C&T Publishing, 1996.

Nadelstern, Paula, "Snowflakes & Quilts." C&T Publishing, 2001.

Newman, Velda, "A Painter's Approach to Quilt Design." Fiber Studio Press, 1996.

Newman, Velda, "A Workshop with Velda Newman." C&T Publishing, 2002.

Olson, Barbara, "Journey of an Art Quilter: Creative Strategies and Techniques." Dragon Threads, 2004.

Pasquini Masopust, Katie, "Ghost Layers and Color Washes." C&T Publishing, 2001.

Shay, Joan, "Petal by Petal." American Quilter's Society, 1998.

Shay, Joan, "Petal Play the Traditional Way." American Quilter's Society, 2001.

Shay, Joan; Bethany Reynolds and Karen Combs, "Three Quilters Celebrate the Four Seasons." American Quilter's Society, 2004.

Smith, Lura Schwarz, "Faces in Fabric" DVD. http://www.jukeboxquilts.com, 2003.

Stuart, Trish, "Portraits of Alaska." Twisted Threads, 2000.

Stuart, Trish, "Grizzlies." Twisted Threads, 2002.

Stuart, Trish, "Quilt Art: Coloring your Quilts." Twisted Threads, 2002.

Stuart, Trish, "Quilt Art: More Quilts to Color." Twisted Threads, 2003.

Stuart, Trish, "Quilt Art: Curves Made Easy." Twisted Threads, 2003.

Tims, Ricky, "Convergence Quilts — Mysterious, Magical, Easy & Fun." C&T Publishing, 2003.

Tims, Ricky, "Quilting Caveman Style" DVD. Autumn Rock Media Productions, 2003.

Wood, Kaye, "6 Hour Quilts", Kaye Wood Inc, 1994.

Wood, Kaye, "Starmaker Design Concepts", Kaye Wood Inc, 1996.

Wood, Kaye, "Easy Hexagon Designs", Kaye Wood Inc, 1998.

Wood, Kaye, "Fantastic Fans", Kaye Wood Inc, 1999.

Wood, Kaye, "Pieces of Eight", Kaye Wood Inc, 2001.

Wood, Kaye, "Circles Made Simple", Kaye Wood Inc, 2002.

Wood, Kaye, "Stars Made Simple", Kaye Wood Inc, 2003.

Wood, Kaye, "Strip Cut Quilts", KP Books, 2002.

Wood, Kaye, "Everyone Can Quilt", KP Books, 2004.

Walter, Cindy, "Snippet Sensations.." KP Books, 1996.

Walter, Cindy and Diana Leone, "Fine Hand Quilting." KP Books, 2000.

Walter, Cindy, and Diana Leone, "Attic Windows." KP Books, 2000.

Walter, Cindy, "More Snippet Sensations." KP Books, 2000.

Walter, Cindy and Jennifer Priestley, "Basic Guide to Dyeing and Painting Fabric." KP Books, 2002.

Walter, Cindy, "Snippet Flower Bouquet." KP Books, 2002.

Walter, Cindy, "Christmas Celebration." KP Books, 2002.

Walter, Cindy, and Gail Rowe, "Basic Applique." KP Books, 2002.

Wasilowski, Laura, "Fusing Fun." C&T Publishing, 2004.

Resources

American Quilter's Society Show
Web site: http://www.Americanquilter.com

Benartex Inc.
(Wholesale only)
1359 Broadway
Suite 1100
New York, NY 10018
Telephone: (212) 840-3250
Web site: http://www.benartex.com

Bernina of America
3702 Prairie Lake Court
Aurora, IL 60504-6182
Web site: http://www.berninausa.com

Bohin France
St. Sulpice Sur Risle BP 212
L Aigle Cedex
61306 France
Web site: http://www.bohin.com

Checker Distributors
(Wholesale only)
Telephone: (800) 537-1060
Web site: http://www.checkerdist.com

Clover Needlecraft
(Wholesale only)
Telephone: (615) 895-0513
Web site: http://www.clover-usa.com

The Colonial Needle Co.
(Wholesale only)
74 Westmoreland Road
White Plains, NY 10606
Phone: (914) 946-7474
Web site: http://www.colonialneedle.com

Country Stitches
2200 Coolidge Road
East Lansing, MI 48823
Telephone: (517) 351-2416
Web site: http://www.countrystitches.com

E.E. Schenck Co.
(Wholesale only)
Maywood Studio
P.O. Box 5200
Portland, OR 97208
Telephone: (503) 284-4124
Web site: http://www.eeschenck.com

Electric Quilt Company
419 Gould St.
Suite 2
Bowling Green, OH 43402
Telephone: (410) 352-1134
Web site: http://www.electricquilt.com

Fairfield Processing Corp.
(Wholesale only)
P.O. Box 1130
Danbury, CT 06813-1130
Telephone: (800) 980-8000
Web site: http://www.poly-fil.com

Fiberactive Quilt Company
(Wholesale, retail maker of patterns)
5917 Oxford Green Drive
Apex, NC 27539
Telephone: (919) 772-1412
Web site: http://www.fiberactivequilts.com

Free Spirit
(Wholesale only)
350 Broadway, 21st floor
New York, NY 10018
Web site: http://www.Freespiritfabric.com

Golden Threads
(Wholesale, retail sale of stencils, quilting line designs, quilting paper)
2 S. 373 Seneca Drive
Wheaton, IL 60187
Telephone: (630) 510-2067
Web site: http://www.Goldenthreads.com

Gütermann of America, Inc.
(Wholesale only)
P.O. Box 7387
Charlotte, NC 28241
Web site: http://www.Gutermann-us.com

Hobbs Bonded Fibers
(Wholesale only)
200 S. Commerce Drive
Waco, TX 76710
Web site: http://www. HobbsBondedFibers.com

Hoffman California International Fabrics
(Wholesale only)
2572 Obrero Drive
Mission Viejo, CA 92691-3140
Telephone: (949) 770-2922

Holiday Designs
683 Laurel Drive
Boiling Springs, PA 17007
Web site: http://www.donnaposter.com

Husqvarna Viking Sewing Machines
White Sewing Machines
31000 Viking Parkway
Westlake, OH 44145
Telephone: (800) 358-0001
E-mail: info@husqvarnaviking.com
Web site: http://www.husqvarnaviking.com

In the Beginning Fabrics
(Wholesale and retail store)
8201 Lake City Way N.E.
Seattle, WA 98115-4476
Web site: http://www.inthebeginningfabrics.com

International Quilt Market and Festival
Quilts Inc.
7660 Woodway Drive, Suite 550
Houston, TX 77063
Web site: http://www.quilts.com

Jacquard Products
Telephone: (800) 442-0455
Web site: http://www.jacquardproducts.com

Kaye Wood Inc.
Telephone: (800) 248-KAYE
Web site: http://www.kayewood.com

Mancuso Quilt Shows
Web site: http://www.quiltfest.com

Michell Marketing, Inc.
3525 Broad St.
Chamblee, CA 30341
Telephone: (770) 458-6500
Web site: http://www.frommarti.com

Milliken
(Wholesale only)
Printed Treasures
E-mail: info@printedtreasures.com

Mountain Mist
(Wholesale only)
2551 Crescentville Road
Cincinnati, OH 45241
Telephone: (800) 345-7150
Fax: (513) 326-3911
E-mail: vickie.paullus@leggett.com
Web site: http://www.mountainmistlp.com

Omnigrid
A Division of Prym Dritz Corp.
P.O. Box 5028
Spartanburg, SC 29304
Telephone: (864) 576-5050

P&B Textiles
1580 Gilbreth Road
Burlingame, CA 94010
Web site: http://www.pbtex.com

Primedia
(Quilter's Newsletter Magazine, McCall's Quilting magazine)
741 Corporate Circle, Suite A
Golden, CO 80401
Web site: http://www.Primedia.com

Quilt Central TV
305 Jefferson St.
Paducah, KY 42001
Telephone: (866) PADUCAH
Web site: http://www.Quiltcentraltv.com

Quilting Arts magazine
P.O. Box 685
Stow, MA 01775
Telephone: (978) 798-9695
Web site: http://www.quiltingarts.com

RJR Fabrics
(Wholesale only)
2203 Dominguez St., Bldg. K-3
Torrance, CA 90505
Telephone: (310) 222-8782
Web site: http://www.rjrfabrics.com

Road to California Quilt Show
Web site: http://www.road2ca.com

Robert Kaufman Co., Inc.
(Wholesale only)
129 W. 132nd St.
Los Angeles, CA 90061
Telephone: (800) 877-2066
Web site: http://www.robertkaufman.com

Rosie's Calico Cupboard
7151 El Cajon Blvd., Suite 'F'
San Diego, CA 92115
Telephone: (619) 697-5758
Fax: (619) 465-8298
Web site: http://www.rosiescalicocupboard.com

Silkworks
5740 Ranger St.
Virginia Beach, VA 23464
Telephone: (757) 424-5893
Web site: http://www.thesilkworks.com

Sulky of America
(Wholesale only)
3113 Broadpoint Dr.
Punta Gorda, FL 33983
Telephone: (800) 874-4115
Web site: http://www.sulky.com

Superior Threads
P.O. Box 1672
St. George, UT 84771
Telephone: (800) 499-1777
Web site: http://www.superiorthreads.com

The Warm Co.
(Wholesale only)
954 East Union St.
Seattle, WA 98122
Telephone: (206) 320-9276
Web site: http://www.warmcompany.com